THE GREAT ARCHAEOLOGISTS

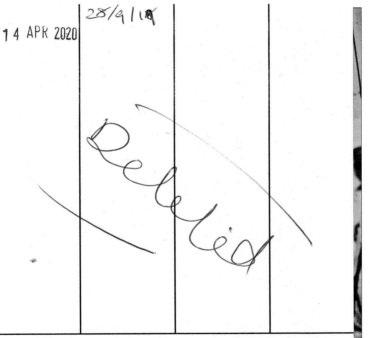

28/9/18

14 APR 2020

Deleted

Books should be returned or renewed by the last date above. Renew by phone **08458 247 200** or online *www.kent.gov.uk/libs*

THE GREAT ARCHAEOLOGISTS

EDITED BY
PAUL BAHN

The lives and legacies of the people who discovered the world's most famous and important archaeological sites, with over 180 stunning photographs

Fabulous tales of extraordinary explorers such as Heinrich Schliemann, the excavator of Troy, and Howard Carter, the discoverer of Tutankhamen's tomb

southwater

This edition is published by Southwater, an imprint of Anness Publishing Ltd, Hermes House, 88–89 Blackfriars Road, London SE1 8HA; tel. 020 7401 2077; fax 020 7633 9499 www.southwaterbooks.com; www.annesspublishing.com

Anness Publishing has a new picture agency outlet for images for publishing, promotions or advertising. Please visit our website www.practicalpictures.com for more information.

UK agent: The Manning Partnership Ltd
   tel. 01225 478444; fax 01225 478440; sales@manning-partnership.co.uk
UK distributor: Grantham Book Services Ltd
   tel. 01476 541080; fax 01476 541061; orders@gbs.tbs-ltd.co.uk
North American agent/distributor: National Book Network
   tel. 301 459 3366; fax 301 429 5746; www.nbnbooks.com
Australian agent/distributor: Pan Macmillan Australia
   tel. 1300 135 113; fax 1300 135 103; customer.service@macmillan.com.au
New Zealand agent/distributor: David Bateman Ltd
   tel. (09) 415 7664; fax (09) 415 8892

Produced for Lorenz Books by Toucan Books
Managing Director: Ellen Dupont

Anness Publishing Limited:
Publisher: Joanna Lorenz
Editorial Director: Helen Sudell
Editor: Elizabeth Woodland

For Toucan Books:
Editor: Jane Chapman
Designer: Elizabeth Healey
Picture researcher: Wendy Brown
Maps: Julian Baker
Proofreader: Marion Dent
Indexer: Michael Dent

Contributors: Dr Paul Bahn (editor and contributor), Dr Caroline Bird (Australasia), Dr Peter Bogucki (prehistoric Europe), Jane Callander (D. Garrod), Dr Philip Duke (North America), Dr Chris Edens (Near East), Dr David Gill (Classical world), Dr Geoffrey McCafferty (Mesoamerica), Dr Jane McIntosh (south Asia), Dr Margarete Pruech (Far East), Dr Anne Solomon (Africa), Dr Joyce Tyldesley (Egypt), Dr Karen Wise (South America).

ETHICAL TRADING POLICY
At Anness Publishing we believe that business should be conducted in an ethical and ecologically sustainable way, with respect for the environment and a proper regard to the replacement of the natural resources we employ.
   As a publisher, we use a lot of wood pulp to make high-quality paper for printing, and that wood commonly comes from spruce trees. We are therefore currently growing more than 750,000 trees in three Scottish forest plantations: Berrymoss (130 hectares/320 acres), West Touxhill (125 hectares/305 acres) and Deveron Forest (75 hectares/185 acres). The forests we manage contain more than 3.5 times the number of trees employed each year in making paper for the books we manufacture.
   Because of this ongoing ecological investment programme, you, as our customer, can have the pleasure and reassurance of knowing that a tree is being cultivated on your behalf to naturally replace the materials used to make the book you are holding.
   Our forestry programme is run in accordance with the UK Woodland Assurance Scheme (UKWAS) and will be certified by the internationally recognized Forest Stewardship Council (FSC). The FSC is a non-government organization dedicated to promoting responsible management of the world's forests. Certification ensures forests are managed in an environmentally sustainable and socially responsible way. For further information about this scheme, go to www.annesspublishing.com/trees

© Anness Publishing Ltd 2008

CONTENTS

INTRODUCTION

Interest in archaeology has never been more popular than it is today, with numerous popular television shows devoted to it and archaeological tourism now is responsible for quite a considerable slice of the economy of many countries, including Egypt, Mexico and Peru.

Archaeology is a truly vast subject, encompassing everything made or done by humans, from the first known stone tools about 2.6 million years ago, up to events in recent history. The whole world is available for study to the archaeologist, barring wars or natural disasters, from mountains to jungle, from remote islands to big cities and from deserts to shipwrecks. Few fields of learning can match this geographical breadth and chronological depth.

This book will take you on a journey back in time and to different cultures and landscapes. It looks at the lives and work of many of the great archaeologists — the men and women whose commitment to uncovering the secrets of the past has brought us face to face with our ancestors.

The early days of archaeology brought a succession of intrepid, often colourful scholars and adventurers. Among them were Arthur Evans and Heinrich Schliemann who gave the modern world its first glimpse of the Minoan and Mycenaean civilizations. There were also early Egyptologists, Giovanni Belzoni and Auguste Mariette; Max Uhle, the father of South American archaeology; and Augustus Pitt Rivers whose meticulous approach to excavation put field work on a more professional footing. Early milestones include the decoding of the Rosetta Stone by Champollion in the early 1820s.

The first professional archaeologists began to emerge in the early 20th century. Their pioneering work led to many significant breakthroughs, such as Alfred Kidder's excavations at Pecos, New Mexico; Dorothy Garrod's studies at the Palaeolithic caves of Mount Carmel; and, in 1922, perhaps the

Above A magnificent gold necklace from a spectacular collection of pre-Hispanic jewellery found in Tomb 7 at Monte Albán, in Mexico. The man who made the discovery was the great Mexican archaeologist Alfonso Caso (1896-1970).

greatest discovery of them all — the tomb of Tutankhamen in Egypt's Valley of the Kings by the English archaeologist Howard Carter.

As the 20th century progressed, archaeology became primarily a field for highly qualified specialists, who had access to new and ever more sophisticated techniques for dating, excavation and survey. The new wave of archaeologists made significant breakthroughs in many subject areas and in every corner of the world. The groundbreaking excavations of several generations of the Leakey family in Africa, for example, have had a significant impact on our understanding of the origins of man. In Peru the tireless dedication of Maria Reiche ensured that the Nasca lines were brought to the attention of the wider world.

Other great landmarks of modern archaeology include the decipherment of Linear B by the English scholar Michael Ventris, Kathleen Kenyon's important discoveries in Jerusalem and Jericho, and the Russian-born Tatiana Proskouriakoff's pioneering studies of the Maya.

This timeline presents a selective list of significant milestones and events in the history of places and civilizations featured in this book.

500,000 BC	**Far East**	* Peking Man, a skeleton found at Zhoukoudian, may date back to this time
130,000 BC	**Africa**	* *Homo sapiens sapiens* develop as a species
50,000 BC	**Oceania**	* The first stone tools in Lake Mungo, Australia, are made * Some of the rock art at Dampier may date back to this time
13,000 BC	**Europe**	* The people of Mezhirich in the Ukraine build shelters out of mammoth bones
5500 BC	**Africa**	* 5500-2500 Saharan rock art is created
5000 BC	**Far East**	* Mehrgarh in Pakistan has become a prosperous town and centre of industry
4000 BC	**Middle East** **Far East**	* The Uruk society reaches its height in the 4th millennium * Harappa in Pakistan is an important centre of the local Harappan Bronze Age culture
3300 BC	**Europe**	* The Iceman found in the Ötztaler Alps lives around this time
3100 BC	**Middle East**	* Development of proto-Elamite script begins at Susa * The Sumerians develop cuneiform in the late 4th and early 3rd millennia
3000 BC	**Africa** **Europe**	* 2975-2950 Distinctive dynastic mastaba tombs are built at Saqqara and Abydos * The first monument at Stonehenge in Wiltshire is constructed
2700 BC	**Africa**	* Djoser (ruled 2668-2649) commissions Egypt's first stone building
2600 BC	**Africa**	* Khufu (ruled 2551-2528) built his Great Pyramid at Giza, the site of many later monuments, such as the Great Sphinx
1700 BC	**Far East** **Mediterranean**	* Foundation of the Shang Dynasty in China * The New Palace at Knossos is built by the Minoans of Crete in the 16th century
1500 BC	**Mediterranean**	* The Mycenaeans of Greece come to prominence
1400 BC	**Africa** **Mediterranean**	* Tutankhamen (ruled 1333-1324) is interred in the Valley of the Kings * A Bronze Age ship sinks off the cape of Ulu Burun in Turkey in the 14th century
1300 BC	**Africa**	* Ramesses II (c.1290-1224) builds the twin temples of Abu Simbel

800 BC	**Mediterranean**	* 776 The alleged date of the first Olympic games at Olympia
	Europe	* Central Europe is inhabited by the Celts
700 BC	**Mediterranean**	* The first temple at Delphi is probably built in the 7th century
	Europe	* The Celtic kingdoms of central Europe begin to show Mediterranean influence
	Americas	* Occupation begins at Tikal, a Mayan city in Guatemala
600 BC	**Middle East**	* Construction of Persepolis begins under Darius the Great (ruled 522-486)
500 BC	**Mediterranean**	* The Temple of Zeus at Olympia is constructed
	Far East	* Rich burials of horse-riding nomads begin in the Altai mountains of Siberia
	Americas	* Construction of the Great Pyramid at Cholula begins
400 BC	**Middle East**	* 330 Alexander the Great destroys the palace at Persepolis
300 BC	**Far East**	* 210 Qin Shi Huangdi, the first Chinese emperor, was buried with over 7000 life-size terracotta soldiers
200 BC	**Mediterranean**	* Eumenes (ruled 197-159) built the Altar of Zeus at Pergamon * 146 Carthage is destroyed by the Romans
AD 1-100	**Mediterranean**	* 64 Nero constructs the Domus Aurea after a fire in Rome * 79 Mount Vesuvius erupts destroying Pompeii and Herculaneum
	Americas	* The Moche culture emerges in coastal northern Peru
AD 500	**Americas**	* The Central Mexican city of Teotihuacán reaches its height in the 6th century
	Europe	* The burial mounds at Sutton Hoo are in use from the late 6th century
AD 600	**Americas**	* The Ancestral Puebloan (Anasazi) Indian society flourishes in Mesa Verde
AD 800	**Americas**	* Occupation begins at the Mayan city of Chichén Itzá
AD 1000	**Americas**	* A group of Scandinavians settle at L'Anse aux Meadows in Newfoundland
AD 1350	**Oceania**	* Shag River Mouth in New Zealand is occupied for about 50 years
AD 1400	**Americas**	* The Chimú are conquered by the Incas and the assimilation of their culture greatly influences the course of Inca civilization
AD 1700	**Oceania**	* HMS *Pandora* sinks in Australia's Great Barrier Reef in the 1790s
AD 1800	**Americas**	* 1876 The Battle of Little Bighorn takes place

FOUNDERS OF ARCHAEOLOGY

During the 19th century, adventurers and antiquarians realized that the secrets of the past, both treasure and knowledge, lay beneath their feet. A cast of sometimes colourful, mostly self-taught amateurs populated archaeology in those years. Each had his style, from the hell-for-leather pursuit of the spectacular find of Schliemann, to Belzoni, who uncovered the Great Temple at Abu Simbel (facing page), and from the single-minded application of Champollion in his quest to decode Egyptian hieroglyphs, to the meticulous, analytical approach to excavation of Pitt Rivers, for whom the everyday was as important as the exotic. Whatever their ways and means, all of these men helped lay the foundations for today's scientific discipline of archaeology, whether by establishing methods, by capturing the public's imagination or simply by inspiring others to follow in their footsteps.

Arthur Evans On the island of Crete, Evans found the remains of Europe's oldest literate civilization, which he named 'Minoan'.

Ephraim George Squier The enigmatic Squier meticulously catalogued the work of the mid-West's so-called Mound Builders.

Max Uhle Known as the father of South American archaeology for his work at Pachácamac and other sites in the Andes.

Giovanni Belzoni

(1778-1823)

After a colourful early career, which included a stint as a strongman in an English circus, this 2m (6ft 7in) giant of a man, Italian by birth, went on to become one of the pioneering figures of Egyptology. Among other achievements, Belzoni uncovered the Great Temple at Abu Simbel.

Born the son of a barber, in Padua in north-eastern Italy, Giovanni Battista Belzoni was peripatetic from the start. At one time he wanted to become a monk, joining a Capuchin monastery, then changed his mind and turned his attention to hydraulic engineering. By his mid-twenties, he was married and living in London, where poverty led him to exploit his exceptional height and strength by working in fairs and

Below Egyptian workers under Belzoni hau the top part of the statue of Ramesses II from the Ramesseum in 1816. The lower sect on of the seated figure remains in situ.

circuses. Also at this time, he first met his future patron, the painter, traveller and antiquarian Henry Salt.

Arriving in Egypt

Belzoni never gave up his interest in hydraulics, however, and in 1815 he visited Egypt, with the aim of selling a new design of water wheel to the pasha (ruler), Mohammed Ali. When this project failed, Belzoni started to work for Salt, recently appointed British consul-general in Cairo.

His first commission was to retrieve the upper section of a colossal statue of Ramesses II for the British Museum

in London, where it remains today. The Italian's engineering skills came into play as he carefully removed the detached head-and-shoulders portion of the figure from the courtyard of the Ramesseum, on the west bank of the Nile opposite modern Luxor, and had it shipped back to England. He then sailed south to visit Abu Simbel. Back in Luxor, he carried out excavations at the Karnak Temple and discovered the tomb of Ay, Tutankhamen's successor.

In February 1817 Belzoni cleared away the deep blanket of sand under which the Great Temple at Abu Simbel had remained buried. In October he

Above Nineteenth-century travellers pose before the ruins of the Ramesseum. The complex, the mortuary temple of Ramesses II, one of Egypt's longest-reigning pharaohs, lies in western Thebes, opposite modern Luxor.

made a string of remarkable finds in the Valley of the Kings: the unfinished tomb of Prince Mentuherkhepshef (a son of Ramesses IX), the tomb of 19th Dynasty founder Ramesses I and the beautifully decorated tomb of his son, Seti I, father of Ramesses II.

Belzoni next worked at Giza, where in 1818 he became the first person in modern times to reach the interior of the Pyramid of Khaefre, the second largest of the pyramids at Giza, whose entrance he had discovered hidden on the north face. He inscribed a message dating his discovery – 2 March 1818 – on the internal wall of the pyramid.

After a journey to the shores of the Red Sea, where he identified the ruins of the Greco-Roman port of Berenice, Belzoni travelled south to the island of Philae, located in the Nile near Aswan, to recover a fallen obelisk on behalf of Englishman William John Bankes. In spite of an altercation with the French Consul, Drovetti, who claimed the column for France, Belzoni succeeded in acquiring it. Bankes erected the obelisk in his garden at Kingston Lacy, Dorset, where it still stands. Belzoni then set out into the Western Desert towards Libya, where he hoped to find the oasis of Jupiter Ammon.

Into print

In 1820 Belzoni published his *Narrative of the Operations and Recent discoveries within the pyramids, temples, tombs and excavations in Egypt and Nubia; and of a journey to the coasts of the Red Sea, in search of the Ancient Berenice; and another in the oasis of Jupiter Ammon*. The work was a bestseller and was followed by a successful exhibition of his finds in the recently completed Egyptian Hall in Piccadilly, London.

In 1822 Belzoni travelled to Russia, where he met Tsar Alexander I. His last adventure was an attempt to reach the fabled city of Timbuktu. But he made it only as far as Benin, west Africa, where he died of dysentery on 3 December 1823, aged 45.

Belzoni operated before the age of scientific archaeology and, judged by its precepts, his methods were open to question. He was more interested in finding monuments than in recording or studying them, and he often caused irreparable damage in the process. He has also been accused of being little more than a 'tomb robber', someone who hunted treasures in order to sell them to European collectors. Even so, his discoveries were groundbreaking and he was an inspiration to future generations of Egyptologists, assuring his place as a pioneer in the field.

J.F. Champollion

(1790-1832)

Champollion was the brilliant young scholar who in the early 1820s cracked the code of the Rosetta Stone. In doing so, he made it possible to solve one of the great academic mysteries of the age — how to decipher the lost language of ancient Egypt — and opened up a new era in Egyptology.

Jean-François Champollion was born less than a year after the start of the French Revolution and grew up in the town of Figeac in south-west France. He was a precocious child and enjoyed studying foreign languages, becoming proficient in many, including Italian, English, Latin, Greek, Arabic, Coptic and Chaldean. In 1809, when only 19, he was appointed assistant professor of history at the Lyceum of Grenoble, where he had been a student.

Given his interest in languages, it was natural that Champollion should become involved in the attempt to decipher ancient Egypt's hieroglyphic script. The French discovery, in 1799, of the Rosetta Stone, a stela (inscribed tablet) dating from the Ptolemaic era, offered a realistic chance of doing that, since it bears a decree written in two languages — Egyptian and Greek — but laid out in three texts. The Greek version uses Greek characters, but the Egyptian text is inscribed in both hieroglyphs and demotic script.

Slowly but resolutely, Champollion pieced together the different portions of the puzzle. By late 1821 he had proved that demotic was a late, much simplified version of hieroglyphs. He had also demonstrated that individual hieroglyphs did not necessarily stand for individual words, suggesting that they had a phonetic component — that some, at least, stood for particular sounds or groups of sounds. He knew too that royal names were written in cartouches (flattened ovals). The latter provided an important lead, enabling

Below The Rosetta Stone, discovered in Rosetta, Egypt, in 1799 by French troops, was the primary key to decoding Egyptian script. This is a detail of its hieroglyphic inscription.

Champollion to read 'Ptolemy' on the Rosetta Stone, both 'Ptolemy' and 'Cleopatra' on the obelisk recovered by Belzoni from the island of Philae and 'Alexander' on an inscription from the Karnak Temple. In this way Champollion was able to create an alphabet of 12 hieroglyphs, each one representing a sound, that could be applied to all Greco-Roman names written in Egyptian.

The puzzle completed

This phonetic solution to hieroglyphs worked with non-Egyptian names, but it was far from clear whether it held for Egyptian ones. The breakthrough came on 14 September 1822. While working on texts from the temples at Abu Simbel, which were 1500 years older than the inscriptions on the Rosetta Stone, and thus old enough to contain traditional Egyptian names, Champollion came across a cartouche that ended in a repeated hieroglyph. According to his phonetic alphabet, the symbol represented the sound of the letter 's', so he surmised that the royal name set down in the cartouche ended in a double 's'. Turning to the remaining two hieroglyphs in the cartouche, he postulated that the disc-shaped symbol at the beginning might represent the sun. In Coptic, a form of ancient Egyptian now used only by the Coptic Church, the word for sun is 'ra'. He then deduced that the second symbol in the cartouche stood for 'm' and that the name was Ramesses.

Fame at last

Champollion immediately presented his discoveries to the Academy of Inscriptions in Paris. Two years later he published a more comprehensive work, *A Summary of the Hieroglyphic System of the Ancient Egyptians*, in which he showed that hieroglyphs could represent sounds as well as concepts, depending on the context. The book

made him a celebrity and was the foundation upon which all further decoding of hieroglyphs was based.

In 1826 Champollion was named curator of the Egyptian collection of the Louvre Museum in Paris, then in 1828 began a year-long tour of Egypt, his first and only visit to the country. Champollion was created professor of archaeology at the Collège de France in Paris in March 1831 but died from a stroke a year afterwards. His ancient Egyptian grammar and dictionary were published posthumously, in 1836 and 1841 respectively.

Right This cartouche represents the name of Seti I. Cartouches similar to this but containing Greco-Roman names set Champollion on the road to deciphering hieroglyphs.

Sir Arthur Evans

(1851-1941)

On Crete, Arthur Evans discovered the remains of Europe's oldest literate civilization and believed that he had found the palace of the legendary King Minos. His interpretation has been derided as wish-fulfilment, yet Evans' methods mark him as a founder of modern field archaeology.

Arthur Evans first visited the island of Crete in 1894 to look for prehistoric coins and seals (clay tablets). As a boy in Hertfordshire, England, Evans had been fascinated by the inscriptions on ancient coins and artefacts collected by his father, Sir John Evans, who was a noted numismatist (coin specialist) and antiquarian. Sir John was also a successful businessman whose wealth enabled his son to first study modern history at Oxford and afterwards tour the Balkans. In 1876 Arthur Evans became special correspondent in the Balkans for *The Manchester Guardian*, and between then and 1882, when he was expelled from the region on political grounds, he identified the sites of several Roman roads and cities in Bosnia and Macedonia.

Below This fresco from 1700-1400 BC, found at Knossos, depicts bull-vaulting, believed to be a religious ritual among the Minoans.

In 1884 Evans took up a post as a keeper of the Ashmolean Museum in Oxford. He believed that a script, as yet undeciphered, on Aegean Bronze Age coins in the collections belonged to the Mycenaeans. He visited Athens to search for similar inscriptions and learnt that on Crete, peasants often unearthed inscribed seals, coins and gemstones when cultivating their fields.

Travels in Crete

Accompanied by a young student, John Myres (later celebrated for his archaeological excavations on Cyprus), Evans travelled through Crete in 1894-5, searching for sites and inscribed artefacts. The two nurtured the idea that the Greek myths were based on historical fact. The previous year Myres had applied for a licence to dig at the tell (artificial mound) at Kephala (Knossos), where in 1878 the Cretan archaeologist Minos Kalokairinos had uncovered sections of a great building. Evans and Myres were not the only ones interested in digging at Kephala at around this time. Heinrich Schliemann was among the others who applied. All were unsuccessful although in 1895 Evans, with money and all the credentials and contacts of a journalist and antiquarian, was allowed to buy part of the site.

Kephala

Arthur Evans began his excavations at 11 a.m. on Friday, 23 March, 1900. He was assisted by David Hogarth and Duncan MacKenzie, experts in archaeological methods, and also by Theodore Fyfe, a specialist in ancient architecture. MacKenzie kept meticulous records of the excavations in his day books. The chambers and storerooms that the team uncovered and the artefacts they discovered there told them that the site was the palace-city of an early literate civilization. However, Evans's interpretations of the finds at the mound were controversial. Basing his deductions on the Homeric myths and

Above This is the smaller of two cult figurines from c.1500 BC discovered close to the central shrine at Knossos. Both figurines hold serpents and may have been snake goddesses.

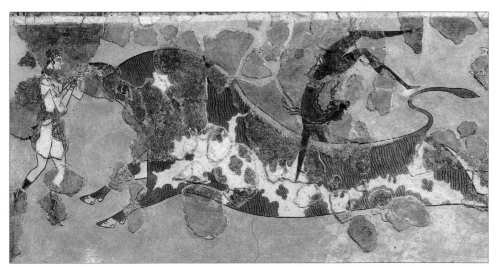

Above Minoan pillars, unlike Greek columns, are wider at the top than the bottom. Evans had many rebuilt and painted to match the plaster he found on some floors and walls.

on coins found at the site, which bore images of labyrinths, minotaurs and of Ariadne, daughter of King Minos, Evans declared that he had found the palace of the mythical Cretan king, who had kept the Minotaur (half man, half bull) in a labyrinth.

Some repair of the site's crumbling walls, stairs and foundations proved necessary for safety and for access to some parts of the complex. However, Evans rebuilt walls and reconstructed rooms using reinforced concrete, rebuilt timber structures and painted his 'reconstitutions', as he referred to them, in pink and terracotta; he also decorated rooms with reproduction frescoes. Evans declared one chamber to be the Throne Room of King Minos and restored it in what he considered to be appropriate style. Archaeologists today avoid such 'over-interpretation' and use of modern materials.

Evans excavated most of the palace complex in four years but lived and worked at Knossos for some 30 years, publishing his findings in four volumes between 1921 and 1931. His views on the site were widely accepted at first,

and in 1911 he received a knighthood. However, his chronology for Minoan civilization clashed with the findings of other archaeologists working in the field and later investigations of the site concluded that the connection with the mythical King Minos was fanciful.

Evans's legacy

Some archaeologists have condemned Evans as a falsifier of history. Yet his achievements outweighed the errors he committed and he was no treasure-seeker. Evans discovered a previously unknown, literate civilization, which dated back beyond the Mycenaeans to the 3rd millennium BC and dominated the Aegean from 1900 to 1300 BC. He remains a towering figure in the development of archaeology, and the names he gave to the site at Kephala that he excavated, 'Knossos', and to the civilization that built it, 'Minoan', continue to be used today.

Above This fresco, known as 'the Prince with Lilies' or 'Priest-King', shows a figure wearing a headdress of lilies and peacock feathers. The fragments of this fresco were discovered beneath the Corridor of the Processions in the south section of the complex at Knossos.

Henry Layard

(1817-1894)

Layard was responsible, along with Frenchman Paul Emile Botta, for the first serious excavations in Mesopotamia (Iraq) and the rediscovery of the Assyrians. Display of his finds in the British Museum and his descriptions of his digs stimulated public enthusiasm for Near Eastern archaeology.

Born in Paris, Layard was the son of an official in the colonial civil service of Ceylon (Sri Lanka). After receiving an education in Europe and Britain, he entered a solicitor's office in London but left six years later with the aim of taking up a post in the Ceylon Civil Service himself. Travelling eastwards overland, Layard got only as far as the Middle East, which he explored thoroughly, visiting numerous ancient sites, including in Iraq various tells (artificial mounds) hiding the ruins of ancient Mesopotamian cities. The tells and the ruins they held fascinated Layard and he developed a desire to

excavate and study them for himself. It was in Iraq that he met Botta, who began excavating in the area of Mosul, in the north of the country, in 1842. That same year Layard's travels took him to Constantinople (Istanbul), the Ottoman capital, where he remained, carrying out unofficial diplomatic tasks for the British envoy, Stratford Canning, until he could fulfil his wish of returning to Iraq to excavate.

Uncovering Assyria

In 1845 Layard secured a gift of £100 from Canning and went back to Iraq to undertake his own excavations. He

began at a site called Nimrud, a tell situated near the banks of the Tigris, 30km (19 miles) south-east of Mosul. On the very first day Layard came across the ruins of an Assyrian palace, and a short time afterwards unearthed a second palace.

During two years of digging, Layard uncovered portions of half a dozen palaces decorated with the limestone wall-reliefs characteristic of Assyrian royal buildings, the colossal statues of human-headed winged bulls that guarded palace portals and numerous smaller works of art. Among the latter was the so-called Black Obelisk, which dated from 825 BC and depicted the military exploits of the Assyrian king Shalmaneser III, including the submission of Jehu, king of ancient Israel, to Assyrian dominion. Layard originally believed that he had found the remains of Nineveh, the Assyrian capital from c.700 BC until its fall in 612 BC. In fact the ruins were those of Kalhu, the biblical city of Calah, which had been the capital of the empire from the 9th century BC until Sargon II moved it north to Dur-Sharrukin (Khorsabad) in 717 BC.

Layard returned home to England in 1847, where his discoveries initially met with mixed reviews. Many people disparaged the aesthetic qualities of

Left A force of local workers moves an Assyrian winged bull statue at the site of Nimrud in 1849. This engraving is taken from Henry Layard's work *Discoveries in the Ruins of Nineveh and Babylon.*

Assyrian art, and the subject was even raised in Parliamentary committee, where the suitability of Layard's finds for display in the British Museum was discussed. Others, meanwhile, among them Layard's patron Canning, were elated. Layard himself sought popular support: his book *Nineveh and Its Remains* (1848-9) placed emphasis on the adventure of archaeology and the biblical associations of his results.

French competition

In 1846 the Louvre Museum in Paris had opened a display of Assyrian finds recovered by Botta, who three years previously had unearthed Sargon II's capital at Khorsabad. Some eminent British figures were not slow in seeing a challenge. Stratford Canning, for one, expressed in a letter to Prime Minister Robert Peel a belief that Layard's Assyrian finds 'will beat the Louvre hollow'. Persuaded by such appeals, the British Museum provided the then considerable sum of £2000 for the archaeologist to ship his finds back to London and continue his work in Mesopotamia. Layard arranged for the artefacts, including carved wall-reliefs and massive winged bulls, to be transported to Britain via India, where curiosity-seekers opened many crates awaiting passage on the quayside. The British Museum opened its Nineveh Gallery in 1853 to popular acclaim.

Layard used the remaining funds to excavate the tell at Kuyunjik, which lay to the east of the Tigris, opposite modern Mosul. In 1849 he uncovered the palace of Sennacherib and tens of thousands of clay tablets from the library of Assurbanipal. The latter find included Mesopotamian literature, dictionaries and other materials that would open the Mesopotamian world to scholarly study. This time there was no mistake: Layard had discovered the ancient city of Nineveh.

In 1849-50 Layard shifted his focus southwards, where he briefly explored Babylon, near modern Al-Hillah, and other mounds. However, used to the immediate results he had enjoyed with the Assyrian tells and unfamiliar with

the technical demands of excavating mud-brick architecture, Layard found these southern sites disappointing. Nevertheless, Layard again presented his findings to a fascinated public in *Discoveries in the Ruins of Nineveh and Babylon*, published in 1853.

A break with the past

Two years previously Layard had left Iraq and abandoned archaeology. In 1852 he entered British politics as Member of Parliament for Aylesbury, subsequently rising to Under Secretary

Above The ruins of the final Assyrian capital of Nineveh were unearthed at Kuyunjik, near Mosul in northern Iraq. Frenchman Paul Emile Botta was the first to excavate at the site, but the breakthrough was made by Layard.

for foreign affairs and being appointed privy counsellor. He served as an MP until 1869, when he traded politics for diplomacy, becoming ambassador first to Spain and later to the Ottoman court in Constantinople, the position formerly held by Layard's one-time patron Stratford Canning.

Auguste Mariette

(1821-1881)

As first Director of Egyptian Monuments, appointed in 1858, Mariette was the most influential Egyptologist of his generation. His achievements included bringing order to the hitherto largely unregulated excavation of the country's antiquities, and the founding of the Egyptian Museum.

A native of Boulogne-sur-Mer on the north coast of France, Mariette spent a brief period in his late teens working in England, first as a schoolmaster and then as a designer for a ribbon-maker. In 1840 he returned to France to complete his education and then took up a teaching position in Boulogne. His fascination with ancient Egypt was triggered in 1842, when he was asked

Below *Mariette's first great discovery was the Serapeum. Here is one of the huge granite sarcophagi in which the bulls were buried.*

to put in order the papers of the recently deceased archaeologist and draughtsman Nestor L'Hôte, a relative who had accompanied Champollion on his 1828 expedition to Egypt. After years of private study of the Coptic and Egyptian languages, in 1847 Mariette published a catalogue of the Egyptian collection in the Boulogne Museum. Two years later, he obtained a junior post at the Louvre Museum.

In 1850 Mariette visited Egypt to collect Coptic manuscripts for the Bibliothèque Nationale. However, he

Above *Ka-aper was a chief lector-priest during the reign of Userkaf (2465-2458 BC). Mariette's workers found the statue near the king's pyramid at Saqqara in 1860.*

found manuscripts in short supply and turned instead to archaeology. His first excavation at Saqqara resulted in the discovery of the Serapeum – the galleries where the sacred bulls of the Apis cult were buried. Mariette went on digging at Saqqara for a further four years before returning to France.

Route to the top

By now an assistant conservator in the Louvre's department of Egyptology, and an archaeologist of some repute,

Right Egyptian workers haul sarcophagi (stone cases) from a tomb, watched over by Mariette (far right). His appointment as the first Director of Egyptian Monuments brought some regulation to the export of artefacts.

Mariette went back to Egypt in 1857 to help to prepare for a visit by Prince Napoleon, a cousin of the French Emperor Napoleon III. He launched a series of excavations at Giza, Saqqara, Abydos, Thebes and Elephantine, where his workmen busily sought out antiquities, which they then reburied so the prince could 'discover' them. The next year the Ottoman viceroy of Egypt, Said Pasha, appointed Mariette to the newly created post of Director of Egyptian Monuments, giving him effective control of the country's antiquities. From then until the end of his life, Egypt was Mariette's home.

Using his near-absolute powers, the new director restricted the selling and export of Egypt's antiquities. In 1859 Mariette persuaded Said Pasha to set up a museum at Bulaq, near Cairo, where they could be preserved. These collections were the basis for today's Egyptian Museum in Cairo, which was eventually opened on its current site in 1902. Mariette also embarked on a massive countrywide programme of simultaneous excavations, employing a force of almost 3000 workers. His projects included the first digs to take place at the Karnak Temple, situated in modern Luxor, as well as a 20-year excavation in the Nile Delta at Tanis, the biblical city of Zoan and a capital of ancient Egypt. In 1859 Mariette's workers found a virtually intact tomb in the necropolis of Dra Abu'l Naga, on the west bank of the Nile at Thebes (opposite Luxor). The treasure-filled coffin within belonged to Ah-hotep, mother of Ahmose I, founder of the 18th Dynasty, among whose pharaohs were Tutankhamen and Akhenaten. The next year Mariette began clearing the temple at Edfu, situated some 96km (60 miles) south of Luxor. The temple had developed into a village over the centuries, with houses having been built even on the sanctuary roof.

Nevertheless, though he nominally excavated at least 35 sites, Mariette was rarely on the spot to supervise his workforce, and the standard of his digs was not high. Additionally, many of his written records were lost when his house at Bulaq flooded in 1878.

Rank and honour

Mariette published a vast range of books and papers, including *Catalogue of the Boulaq Museum* (1864-76), *The Serapeum of Memphis* (1857) and *Karnak* (1875). He also received numerous honours, among them the Légion d'Honneur in 1852 and acceptance into the Académie des Inscriptions et des Belles-Lettres in 1878; in Egypt he was elevated to the rank of bey and later to that of pasha. In addition to his many accomplishments in Egyptology, he also collaborated on the libretto of Verdi's Egyptian-themed opera, *Aïda*, first performed in 1871 in Cairo.

Mariette died in 1881, having been in poor health for some years, and was interred in a sarcophagus at Bulaq. With the completion of the Egyptian Museum in Cairo in 1902, the coffin was moved to the building's forecourt and remains there, surmounted by a bronze statue of the former Director of Egyptian Monuments, which was unveiled in 1904.

Jacques de Morgan
(1857-1924)

Frenchman de Morgan began his working life as a mining engineer but combined this work with a strong and growing interest in archaeology. He eventually abandoned engineering when he accepted the appointment of Director-General of the Egyptian Antiquities Service.

The son of a mining engineer, Jacques de Morgan was born near the town of Blois in north-western France. His father bequeathed him not only his professional leanings but also his avid interest in prehistory. De Morgan graduated from the School of Mines in 1882 and began a career that took him to many parts of northern Europe and Asia. While managing a copper mine in Russian Armenia, he studied early

Below A photograph taken in the 1950s of the 1897 French excavation site at Susa. The project unearthed some remarkable finds, but the approach used meant that all archaeological context was lost.

metallurgy in the Caucasus. He then headed a scientific mission to Persia (Iran), where he combined geological studies – he was the first person to recognize the presence of petroleum in the south-west of the country – with archaeological inquiry.

Late in 1891 de Morgan returned to France but the following year took up the post of Director-General of the Egyptian Antiquities Service, which he held until 1897. While in Egypt, he founded the Greco-Roman Museum in Alexandria and laid the cornerstone of the Cairo Museum. He also carried out some field work, including a brief exploration of Naqada, a prehistoric

site about 24km (15 miles) north of modern Luxor, and the excavation of several pyramids at Dahshur, where he found a trove of royal jewellery dating from ancient Egypt's Middle Kingdom (*c*.1975-1640 BC).

A move to Persia

In 1897 de Morgan was appointed director of the Délégation en Perse, a permanent mission formed to exploit the archaeological research monopoly that Persia had granted France two years earlier. He decided to focus on the ancient city of Susa in the winters and pass the summers in north-west Iran exploring prehistoric cemeteries. His work in the Caucasus shows he could be a competent prehistorian, but he was not prepared for Susa. Deciding that stratigraphic excavation (layer-by-layer analysis) would not be possible, he treated Susa as a 'strip-mining' exercise. Employing a team of 1200 labourers, he removed huge quantities of earth – according to one estimate, 2.45 million cubic metres (86.5 million cubic feet) in less than a decade. As a result, he recovered some superb pieces of Mesopotamian art, including the Victory Stela of Naram-Sin and the Law Code of Hammurabi, but entirely without archaeological or architectural context.

In 1907 he turned over direction of the Susa dig and in 1912 resigned from the Délégation. Returning to France he devoted the remainder of his life to writing such works as the three-volume *La préhistoire orientale*.

Edouard Piette

(1827-1906)

Edouard Piette was a pioneering prehistorian in 19th-century France, who ruined himself financially with his excavations of Palaeolithic cave sites in the south-west of the country. He also amassed the finest collection of Ice Age portable art objects, including the 'Lady of Brassempouy'.

Piette was a lawyer by profession and worked as a provincial magistrate for most of his life. Born at Aubigny in the Ardennes, in north-eastern France, he developed a strong interest in geology at an early age. While a student of law in Paris, he was able to indulge this passion by attending geology lectures at the Sorbonne and at the School of Mines. From geology, his scope soon spread to archaeology and prehistory, especially in the French Pyrenees.

Cave sites in the Pyrenees

Although he carried out important work on tumuli (burial mounds) and monuments of later prehistory, Piette is especially remembered for his pioneering excavations at much earlier sites, such as the caves at Lortet, Arudy, Gourdan and, in particular, Le Mas-d'Azil – all of which are in or near the Pyrenees. At Le Mas-d'Azil, in the foothills of the central part of the range, he first identified a phase in prehistory between the end of the Ice Age and the start of the Neolithic period. Characterized by flat bone harpoons and small pebbles decorated with red dots and stripes, the culture came to be known as the Azilian.

Like other scholars of the period, Piette did not excavate himself but employed workmen to do it, checking them from time to time. He was, nonetheless, a pioneer in many other ways. Not only was he the first scholar to help fill the 'hiatus' after the Ice Age, but he was also one of the first

to find sites by searching systematically in suitable parts of the landscape. He was remarkably open-minded, willing to explore concepts such as the possibility that Palaeolithic people had already started cultivating plants and had succeeded in at least semi-domesticating horses. Piette was one of the very few prehistorians to believe Sanz de Sautuola's claims that figures of

animals in the Altamira cave in northern Spain were painted during the Palaeolithic period. He was also largely responsible for introducing the young Abbé Henri Breuil to the field of prehistory: Piette employed Breuil to produce illustrations of some of his portable art objects.

The beautiful 'Lady'

Piette died in 1906, shortly before the publication of *L'Art Pendant l'Age du Renne* (1907), a magnificent volume devoted to his collection of Ice Age portable art. Even though his research and excavations had left him ruined financially, Piette bequeathed his art collection to the French nation. As well as numerous fine pieces that he had found himself, it also contained items he had acquired from others. Among its best-known pieces is the 'Lady of Brassempouy', a tiny but exquisite carving of a female head, fashioned from a mammoth tusk. Dating from about 21,000 BC, it was found in 1894 in the Grotte du Pape, a cave at Brassempouy in the foothills of the Pyrenees. The statuette can be seen at the National Museum of Antiquities at Saint-Germain-en-Laye near Paris.

Left The 'Lady of Brassempouy', also known as the 'Lady with the Hood', is a statuette standing 3.6cm (1½in) high. It is one of the earliest known examples of a sculpture of the human face – a generalized representation rather than the portrait of an individual.

Augustus Pitt Rivers

(1827-1900)

Nearly 40 years in the British army equipped Pitt Rivers with a military precision, which he brought to the field of archaeology. He established new standards in excavations, insisting on keeping meticulous records of exactly where artefacts were found and the prompt publication of results.

Archaeological excavations during the 19th century were largely unscientific affairs. Diggers often paid little attention to recording the positions of artefacts in the ground, and haphazard methods of excavation prevented accurate logging of the soil layers and the collection of other key information. Furthermore, published documentation was very scarce. It took a retired

Below Pitt Rivers (standing on the top of the mound) supervises the excavation of Wor Barrow on his estate in 1893-4. This long barrow was a Neolithic burial site.

British army general, known to us by his inherited name of Pitt Rivers, to begin to place archaeological field research on a professional footing.

A military career

Pitt Rivers was born Augustus Henry Lane Fox in Hope Hall, Yorkshire, the son of a British military officer. In 1841 he entered the Royal Military Academy at Sandhurst and embarked on his own army career, receiving a commission in the Grenadier Guards in 1845. He was a soldier for almost 40 years, serving in England, Canada,

Ireland, the Crimea and Malta. Lane Fox retired in 1882 with the rank of lieutenant general.

During his military service, Lane Fox began to collect artefacts from the places in which he was stationed. He started by acquiring weapons and then extended his collecting to a broader range of objects, both practical and decorative. His interest went beyond simple acquisition; he was concerned with charting the development down through the ages of practical objects, among them the rifle, a field of study he described as 'typology'.

Left Pitt Rivers was an avid collector throughout his adult life. The items shown here were all found by the 'father of scientific archaeology' and are a jar from London, a Bronze Age axe (below left) and a Neolithic flint axe from Farnham, Dorset.

As his army career went on, Lane Fox also began to excavate archaeological sites and to make detailed notes about his work. Beginning in Ireland in the early 1860s, when he was in his 30s, he investigated sites of many different periods in Brittany, southern England, Wales and even Denmark. In general, Lane Fox worked alone or with a few chosen companions and, from time to time, with hired workers.

In 1880, in his early 50s, Lane Fox inherited an estate of 3500 ha (8650 acres) as well as a large annual income of about £20,000 under the will of his great uncle, Henry Pitt, the second Lord Rivers. The terms of the will required Lane Fox to assume the name of Pitt Rivers; they also enabled him to retire comfortably. His estate spread out over a large expanse of chalk downland in the south of England. Called Cranbourne Chase, it lies where the counties of Hampshire, Dorset and Wiltshire meet. In medieval times, the area had been a royal hunting ground and, until the 19th century, farming there was strictly limited, which meant that any archaeological sites on the estate, such as barrows (burial mounds), had survived largely untouched.

Excavating the Chase

Recognizing the archaeological riches of his land and the neighbouring parts of Cranbourne Chase, Pitt Rivers devoted the rest of his life to their meticulous excavation. He worked on dozens of Bronze Age barrows, as well as investigating several Bronze Age, Iron Age, Roman and Romano-British enclosures. To help him, he had a staff of draughtsmen, surveyors, foremen, excavators and clerks — all labouring under the retired general's demanding and eccentric personality. Pitt Rivers's techniques were ahead of their time, setting standards for documentation and publication that established the foundations upon which archaeology developed in the twentieth century. The results of this work appeared in four imposing volumes, *Excavations in Cranbourne Chase*, published between 1887 and 1898.

Safe pair of hands

When the appointment of Inspector of Monuments was introduced in 1882, Pitt Rivers became the first to hold it, and approached the task of cataloguing and protecting Britain's archaeological sites with customary meticulousness. Despite the fact that his own archaeological research was overshadowed by spectacular finds made elsewhere during his lifetime, such as those of Schliemann at Troy and Mycenae, which had not benefited from such a painstaking approach, Pitt Rivers's contribution to archaeological method came to be appreciated in the decades after his death. A particular disciple was Sir Mortimer Wheeler, himself a military man, who hailed the excavation principles used by Pitt Rivers as the inspiration for his own field work. Pitt Rivers died on 4 May 1900, at the age of 73.

The Pitt Rivers Museum

In 1884, sixteen years before his death, Pitt Rivers gave a collection of about 20,000 archaeological and ethnographic artefacts to the University of Oxford. Today, the Pitt Rivers Museum is one of the world's most remarkable museums, organized by artefact function rather than period or region. This means that all artefacts with a particular purpose can be seen together. The museum's collections have now expanded to include more than 250,000 objects.

Above The fascinating collections at the Pitt Rivers Museum in Oxford give the visitor an insight into how different cultures overcame similar problems.

Above Like the items at the top of the page, this Anglo-Saxon pot, found by Pitt Rivers, is part of a collection that was acquired by the Salisbury and South Wiltshire Museum in 1975.

Henry Rawlinson

(1810-1895)

Soldier, politician and Orientalist, Henry Creswicke Rawlinson was also a noted linguist, whose work from the 1830s to the 1850s on the inscriptions at Behistun helped to decode the cuneiform scripts and make possible the study of the writings of the ancient Mesopotamian world.

Born in the north Oxfordshire village of Chadlington, Rawlinson joined the East India Company as an officer cadet in 1827. Five years later he was posted to Persia (Iran) to help reorganize the Shah's army. During his two years in Persia, he acquired and developed the fascination with cuneiform scripts that would last the rest of his life.

Until the 1830s comparatively little progress had been made in decoding cuneiform scripts, partly for lack of a key like Egypt's Rosetta Stone, a text in several languages, one of which could already be read. Rawlinson and a number of other scholars eventually created that key with their work on the long cuneiform texts that the Persian king Darius I (reigned 521-486 BC) had had inscribed on his tomb near Persepolis and on a cliff at Behistun in western Iran. This text was written in three tongues: Elamite (the language of Susa), Akkadian (the language of Babylon and the Assyrians) and Old Persian. Rawlinson began copying the Behistun inscription in 1835 but had completed only the Old Persian and Elamite versions of the text when tensions between Britain and Persia obliged him to leave.

Another in the field

Rawlinson was not the only scholar attempting to decipher the cuneiform scripts, but he undertook much of his early work in isolation. In 1838 he published the still incomplete results of his work on the Old Persian text from Behistun, unaware of the more successful efforts of the Irish cleric Edward Hincks, who was the first to present the Old Persian cuneiform alphabet. In 1840 Rawlinson, went to Kandahar in Afghanistan as political agent but gained a transfer to Turkish Arabia, where he was British Resident in Baghdad from 1843 to 1849. From Baghdad, Rawlinson was able in 1847 to copy the Akkadian text at Behistun, and in 1851 he published a translation of the first column of the Akkadian version, plus the systematic reading of 246 signs. This was a stunning and decisive breakthrough.

The Akkadian cuneiform was more complicated than the Old Persian. It was a syllabic script, with numerous logograms (signs representing whole words). Sceptics doubted the claims of Rawlinson and others that they had decoded it. In 1857, the Royal Asiatic Society put these doubts to rest. The society placed a newly discovered text before four scholars, among them Rawlinson and Hincks, who returned basically similar translations.

Though known chiefly as a linguist, Rawlinson also undertook some field archaeology. In 1851, having given a collection of Near Eastern antiquities to the British Museum, he received funding from the museum to continue Henry Layard's explorations in Iraq. Retiring from the East India Company in 1855, Rawlinson served as a crown director of the company. He also held a number of diplomatic and cultural posts, including a trusteeship of the British Museum, and was an MP in the 1850s and 1860s.

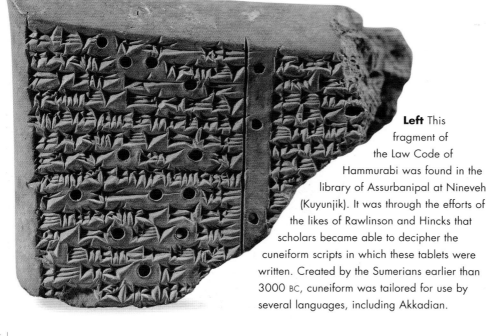

Left This fragment of the Law Code of Hammurabi was found in the library of Assurbanipal at Nineveh (Kuyunjik). It was through the efforts of the likes of Rawlinson and Hincks that scholars became able to decipher the cuneiform scripts in which these tablets were written. Created by the Sumerians earlier than 3000 BC, cuneiform was tailored for use by several languages, including Akkadian.

Sanz de Sautuola

(1831-1888)

Don Marcelino Sanz de Sautuola will forever be linked with the cave of Altamira in Cantabria, northern Spain, whose huge coloured wall and ceiling decorations dating from the Ice Age led him to realize that Palaeolithic people had produced great works of art.

Born in the coastal city of Santander, the capital of the region of Cantabria in northern Spain, Sanz de Sautuola trained as a lawyer. Nevertheless, as a prominent landowner, he did not need to work and was able to devote his time to his numerous interests, among them geology, botany and prehistory.

The marvellous find

In 1876 Sanz de Sautuola paid a visit to a hill called Altamira, which lay on land owned by his family. He had been informed of the existence of a cave by local farmer Modesto Cubillas, who while out hunting eight years earlier had followed his dog into an opening in the hillside, only to discover a series of chambers and passages. During his 1876 visit Sanz de Sautuola noticed some black painted signs on a wall but paid them little attention. In 1879 he returned to do some excavating, and while he was digging in the cave floor for prehistoric tools and portable art of the kind he had not long ago seen displayed at a Paris exhibition, his five-year-old daughter Maria was playing in the cavern. Suddenly, she spotted a number of coloured paintings of animals on the ceiling.

Her father was utterly dumbstruck. He found that the figures seemed to have been created with a fatty paste and noticed the similarity in style between these huge depictions (the red deer is 2.2m/7ft 3in long) and the smaller portable figures he had seen in Paris. He therefore deduced that both types of art were of a similar age, but when he attempted to convince the academic establishment, his ideas met with widespread rejection. Indeed, so well preserved were the paintings that he was even accused of forgery. In 1902, academia recanted and declared that Sanz de Sautuola had been right. Sadly, the news came too late for the Spaniard, who died in 1888, a sad and disillusioned man.

Below The Altamira paintings date from c.14,000-12,000 BC. The animals depicted include bison, horses and deer.

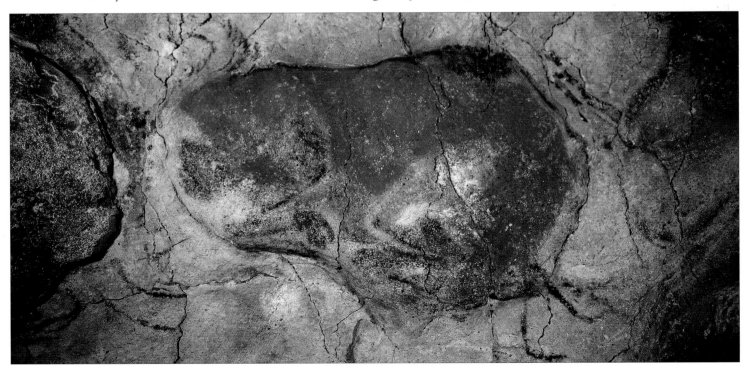

Heinrich Schliemann

(1822-1890)

Self-made businessman and self-taught archaeologist, Schliemann defied the opinions of experts and proved that places described by Homer had existed. By 1873 he had unearthed the site of Troy, and in 1876 he brought to light the Bronze Age civilization of Mycenae.

Schliemann was born into the large family of a poor Protestant minister in the Duchy of Mecklenberg-Schwerin in northern Germany. He mantained that his father imbued in him a love of Homer, which seeded his desire to find the ruins of Troy. This claim may have been wishful thinking, because records show that after the death of Schliemann's mother, his father sent him away, aged 11, to a fee-paying school in a neighbouring duchy. Only months later, though, he had to leave, his father having been accused of embezzling church funds. He then attended a vocational school until, at 14, he was apprenticed to a grocer.

At the age of 19, Schliemann signed on as a cabin boy to work his passage to the Americas but was shipwrecked and washed up in Holland. He was taken on by a commodities company and later by an import/export firm, where he displayed acute judgement and a flair for languages. He was sent to St Petersburg as an agent, then in 1851 sailed for California, where he set up in banking, buying and reselling gold dust from prospectors. In 1852 he returned to Russia, cornered the market in indigo, then moved into munitions when the Crimean War began. By his early forties, having made his fortune three times over, he had retired from business.

Troy and Mycenae

Free of the need to work, Schliemann travelled widely and, in 1868, while on a visit to Ottoman Turkey, he met Frank Calvert, a British archaeologist and consular official. Some historians surmise that Schliemann's obsession with proving the historical existence of Troy, then thought to have existed only in legend, may have emerged at this point. For 20 years Calvert had believed that a tell (artificial mound) at Hissarlik in Turkey was the site of Troy but could not raise the funds to excavate it. Schliemann became his financial partner and, after writing a thesis in support of Calvert's ideas, took over his excavations. He began

Below Schliemann's second wife, Sophia, wears the 'Jewels of Helen', part of the cache known as 'Priam's Treasure', found in the 1870s at Level II of the excavation at Troy.

digging in 1871 and soon found that several cities lay beneath the mound at progressively lower levels. Reasoning that Homeric Troy must be the city at the bottom, Schliemann dug through the ruins of later cities – destroying much archaeological evidence as he went. Later Wilhelm Dörpfeld would divide the site at Hissarlik into nine levels, with Level I, the oldest, at the bottom. In the event, Schliemann got down to Level II, and believed he had uncovered Homeric Troy.

Priam's Treasure

By 1873 Schliemann had unearthed not only the remains of a fortified city but also a spectacular treasure of gold and jewellery. This he believed to be the treasure of King Priam, ruler of Troy during the war against Greece, immortalized in Homer's epic *Iliad*. However, controversy overshadowed his discovery of the treasure, since Schliemann, possibly with Calvert's cooperation, smuggled it out of the country. Schliemann published an account of his excavations in 1874. It was met with a mixture of acclaim and scepticism: archaeologists disparaged both his destructive methods and his fanciful theories. Indeed, Level II at Hissarlik was later dated to about 2500-2300 BC, a thousand years too early for the Troy of the *Iliad*, which has been placed at Level VI/VII.

Schliemann, meanwhile, had a new project. He determined to prove the claim of Pausanias, a geographer of the 2nd century AD, that Agamemnon, who led the Greek attack on Troy, was buried at the hilltop site of Mycenae. He selected a site just inside the gate of the citadel and in August 1876, under the supervision of the Greek Archaeological Society, began digging. Within a month he had uncovered the first of several tombs of Bronze Age chieftains in what is now labelled 'Grave Circle A'. Five wore gold face masks and each had been buried with spectacular weapons, ornaments and vessels of precious metals. Schliemann announced that he had discovered the tombs of Agamemnon, Cassandra and Eurymedon, and the finest of the five masks became known as 'the face of Agamemnon'. Once again, however, these finds were later found to be too old, this time by 300 years.

Troy and Mycenae were not the whole sum of Schliemann's projects. In 1868 he excavated on Ithaca, the legendary island home of Odysseus in the Ionian Sea, and in 1884 he dug at

Tiryns, the Mycenaean hill fort whose ruins Pausanius had visited. Yet Schliemann went back time and again to reopen his site at Troy: in 1878 when he found two more small caches of treasure; again in 1882; and finally in 1888, two years before his death in Naples from an ear infection.

Schliemann's reputation suffered as a result of his damaging excavation methods, dubious site interpretations, lawsuits resulting from his theft of ancient grave goods, and the untruths in his autobiographical writings. He has even been accused of forging some of the treasures he claimed to have found and has often been dismissed as a treasure-seeker. Yet archaeologists today grant his claim to have 'opened up a new world for archaeology' and pay tribute to his determination, energy and dedication – he funded all his excavations – in furthering and publicizing archaeology.

Above This gold chalice with rosette decoration was recovered from Tomb IV of Grave Circle A at Mycenae in Greece and has been dated to the 16th century BC.

Below This photograph from the turn of the 20th century shows sightseers examining Grave Circle A, uncovered by Schliemann in 1876 amid the ruins of Mycenae.

Ephraim Squier

(1821-1888)

Employed variously as journalist, political official and diplomat, Squier is one of the most enigmatic figures in the history of American archaeology. His major work was to catalogue and classify for posterity the prehistoric earthen mounds of the mid-West, many of which are now lost.

Born in Bethlehem, New York, Squier was the son of a Methodist minister. After flirting with civil engineering, education and the law, he became a journalist, editing various publications in New York State, Connecticut and Ohio. He then entered the political world as clerk to the latter state's House of Representatives. While living in the mid-West, Squier became one of the best-known antiquaries in America for his work on the 'Mound Builders'.

The mid-Western states are famous for the many earthen mounds that dot the landscape. These mounds reach back to the prehistoric period, some as far back as the 4th millennium BC,

and had a variety of functions: some were burial sites, for instance, while others were religious in nature. The site of the ancient city of Cahokia in Illinois, inhabited from about AD 700-1400, has mounds of many shapes, the largest of which is believed to have supported the chief's residence; Great Serpent Mound in Ohio is, as its name suggests, in the shape of a snake.

Enter Ephraim Squier

Squier's contribution to the discussion over the origins of these earthworks was the publication in 1848 of *Ancient Monuments of the Mississippi Valley*, a landmark in American scientific research whose byline he shared with

local antiquarian E.H. Davis, although he was responsible for most of the writing. This volume was unique in its comprehensiveness and its accuracy in describing and drawing the mounds, for its meticulous classification of the different categories of mounds and the detailed descriptions of the artefacts and their art styles. Squier felt that the mounds had been built by a lost race of Mound Builders – not the ancestors of contemporary Native Americans as some had postulated. Indeed, it was the prevailing view at the time that the forerunners of the Native Americans would have been incapable of such feats of engineering. The book made him a household name. Furthermore, since so many of the sites he described have since disappeared as a result of development, the volume is invaluable to modern archaeologists.

In 1848 Squier's support for newly elected president Zachary Taylor led to his being appointed US chargé d'affaires in Central America. While he was there, he published works on the region's monuments as well as on its peoples. Squier was able to extend his study of ancient monuments to South America when President Lincoln sent him to Peru as US commissioner in 1862. He returned to New York six years later and in 1873 was divorced. During his life he suffered periodic bouts of mental illness until his death in 1888.

Left The Alligator in central Ohio is one of a number of mounds in the shape of an animal.

Thomsen and Worsaae

(1788-1865 and 1821-1885)

Long before the age of scientific archaeology, Christian Jurgensen Thomsen, curator of the Danish National Museum, and his one-time assistant Jens Jacob Asmussen Worsaae instigated and developed the Three-Age System, still the framework for organizing Eurasian prehistory.

Above This cremation urn lid, from Bronze Age Denmark, is thought to depict the marriage of the god and goddess of fertility.

Thomsen was born in Copenhagen, Denmark, following his father into the family wholesale business. When his parents died, he sold up and devoted himself to his antiquarian interests. In 1816, despite his lack of training, he was entrusted with the curatorship of the nation's Collection of Northern Antiquities, later to develop into the Danish National Museum.

His appointment occurred because by the start of the 19th century, it was clear to scholars throughout most of

Europe that ancient objects lay in the soil. Collections of artefacts began to develop as the activities of farming and industry disturbed many sites. With a view to conserving its wealth of material, Denmark set up a Royal Committee for the Preservation and Collection of National Antiquities, which in turn appointed Thomsen.

Based in the loft of Trinitatis Church in Copenhagen, Thomsen sought to bring order to the chaotic collections and figure out a logical way to display them. He chose to classify the cutting tools according to the material used to make them: stone, bronze and iron. This way of working was not new, but Thomsen extended the classification

to the other materials that were found along with the tools. Certain types of pottery, for example, were associated only with stone implements, while glass beads were found only with iron tools. In this way Thomsen was able to impose order on the collections and propose a chronological scheme: the Stone Age, succeeded by the Bronze Age, followed by the Iron Age. Today we call this the 'Three-Age System'.

One step further

Worsaae, born in Vejle, Denmark, was an assistant to Thomsen from 1838 to 1843 and his successor as the National Museum's curator. Worsaae extended the Three-Age System from museum displays into the field, using layer-by-layer excavation to demonstrate its validity. Some have called Worsaae the 'first professional archaeologist' for his analytical approach to excavation and the study of finds. As a result of his work Thomsen's Three-Age System was adopted throughout Europe.

The Three-Age System still survives as a convenient organizing principle of Eurasian prehistory, and the Stone and Iron Age categories are also applied in Africa. While it is not considered to be an inevitable progression of cultural and technological development, and many of the most interesting times straddle the ages, it still provides a set of basic chronological markers.

Below This burial site north of Alborg, Denmark, dates back as far as the Germanic Iron Age (AD 400-800), which was the final phase of the Iron Age in Northern Europe.

Max Uhle

(1856-1944)

It is impossible to study the ancient civilizations of the Andes without coming across the work of Max Uhle. He brought scientific methods to South American archaeology and formed the basis for our understanding of the relationships of the region's ancient peoples.

Uhle was born in the city of Dresden in eastern Germany. Archaeology did not exist as a discipline when he was growing up and studying, and in 1880 he received his Ph.D. at the University of Leipzig in linguistics; his thesis was on Chinese grammar. Uhle then found work in a Dresden museum, where he came into contact with archaeological objects from around the world. In particular he got the chance to study a range of pieces from the Andes, which were flowing into Germany at that time along with people fleeing the 1879-1884 War of the Pacific between Chile, Bolivia and Peru. Meanwhile, a geologist friend, Alphons Stübel, provided him with data from the ruined city of Tiwanaku (Tiahuanaco) in Bolivia, including photographs and moulds, as well as measurements of architectural features.

After studying the Americas from afar and publishing on Tiwanaku and other aspects of the archaeology of the region, Uhle eventually visited South America in the early 1890s. It was the beginning of a prolific career as a field archaeologist during which he became one of the most important figures in the study of the ancient civilizations of the Americas. Uhle's work was critical both to establishing a number of the main stylistic sequences of Andean archaeology, including those of Nasca

Below Uhle was instrumental in showing that Tiwanaku, Bolivia was a pre-Inca site. This is the ruins' Kalasasaya mound.

and Tiwanaku, and to our knowledge of the archaeological sequence of Andean South America.

First studies

Uhle's early archaeological projects included explorations in Argentina, Bolivia and Chile. His research at Tiwanaku helped establish it as one of the most important pre-Inca cities in the region, and also convinced the Bolivian government to protect what is now one of their most important tourist destinations. It was his analysis of the styles and content of the images on the stonework at Tiwanaku, based on the material brought back by his geologist friend Stübel, that showed that the site predated the Inca. Uhle's identification of similar styles in pottery and other artefacts found at Pachácamac and other sites in coastal Peru laid the groundwork for the timeline of Andean archaeology in use today, although that has been greatly refined in the past century.

Another of Uhle's analyses that has withstood the test of time is his 1917 classification of the mummies of the ancient Chinchorro people, a small-scale society of fishers and hunters of the coastal Atacama desert. Uhle came across the mummies during a visit to northern Chile and he arranged them into three types – simple, complex, simple but clay-covered – a system which is still in use. Since chronometric dating techniques were not available to Uhle in those days, he had no idea how old the mummies were. Later work showed that they are the world's oldest artificially prepared mummies, predating those of ancient Egypt by around 2000 years.

Above These human remains were unearthed in 2005 in an Inca cemetery in Pachácamac, a sacred site first excavated by Uhle in 1896.

However, Uhle's best-known work was on the site of Pachácamac, now an important tourist destination around 40km (25 miles) south of Lima, Peru. A vast settlement built of mud brick but with some stone architecture, it housed one of the most sacred shrines of the Andes under the Inca. Uhle's excavations at Pachácamac included painstaking analysis and documentation of the soil layers, in which he was able to identify several different styles of pottery. He argued that the variations in style represented different periods

Left Among the artefacts given up by Tiwanaku is this incense burner in the form of a puma, for use in religious ceremonies.

of occupation. This work was not only a rich source of data but also produced fabulous and important archaeological collections. Furthermore, it laid the groundwork for the ongoing study of Pachácamac and the chronological and geographical relationships of different archaeological cultures.

Widely considered to be the 'father of South American archaeology', Uhle nevertheless published little. His few works include *The Ruins of Tiahuanaco in the Highlands of Ancient Peru* (with Stübel, 1891) and *Pachácamac: Report of the William Pepper, M.D., LL.D., Peruvian Expedition of 1896* (1903).

PIONEERS OF ARCHAEOLOGY

The early 20th century saw the emergence of a new breed of archaeologists, the first true professionals. Their methods were fast becoming more rigorous and careful than those of their predecessors, and they laid the foundations for the scientific and painstaking approach of our own times. Many of the scholars of the period – Carter, Petrie, Wheeler, Woolley – are among the greatest names in the history of the subject; some of archaeology's most famous discoveries, such as Machu Picchu, the tomb of Tutankhamen, the burials of Ur and the Indus city of Mohenjo-Daro (facing page), are owed to their skill and luck. The first great women archaeologists also came to the fore – Dorothy Garrod and Gertrude Caton-Thompson, for example. The arsenal of techniques available for studying the past also expanded dramatically, with the arrival of aerial photography, pollen analysis and eventually radiocarbon dating.

Henri Breuil During his lifetime, this French archaeologist was considered the foremost authority on Palaeolithic cave art.

Gertrude Caton-Thompson Her excavations at Great Zimbabwe were to challenge western notions of African culture.

Max Mallowan The husband of Agatha Christie. He made important contributions to Mesopotamian archaeology.

Hiram Bingham

(1875-1956)

One of the best-known names in Andean archaeology, Hiram Bingham brought Machu Picchu to the attention of the world. Today, the once lost city of the Inca, perching on the eastern slopes of the Andes, is the most visited site in South America.

Hiram Bingham III was born and raised in Hawaii, the son and grandson of missionaries. He attended Yale University as an undergraduate and then returned for a time to Hawaii. He began graduate studies at the University of California before moving to Harvard, where he studied History and Political Science, obtaining a Ph.D. in 1905. Bingham returned to Yale as an adjunct professor in 1907.

In 1899 Bingham had married Alfreda Mitchell, an heiress and granddaughter of Charles L. Tiffany, founder of the New York jewellery and luxury goods store. His wife's wealth would be important in allowing him to pursue his research interests in South America.

Bingham first travelled to South America in 1906, visiting historical sites in Venezuela and Colombia, and then Argentina and Peru. He attended the first Pan-American Scientific Congress in Chile in 1908, later visiting Cuzco, Peru, the ancient capital of the Inca. He became interested in the early colonial Inca and particularly in finding the lost Inca city of Vilcabamba, where Inca royalty had held out against the Spanish Conquistadors for several years.

A spectacular discovery

Bingham set out for South America again in 1911. With the help of local historians he studied colonial documents and began exploring archaeological ruins along the Urubamba Valley (now known as the Sacred Valley of the Inca) outside Cuzco. On 24 July 1911 he was led by a local guide through the jungle and up a steep path to a spectacular set of Inca ruins located in a spot known as Machu Picchu (Old Mountain Peak). Believing he had found the ruins of Vilcabamba, Bingham announced the discovery of the site and received funding from the National Geographic Society for additional research.

Bingham assembled a team of scholars and scientists to assist him in a multidisciplinary study of the important site. On two subsequent expeditions he cleared, documented and excavated the site. Although his excavation methods were limited, he produced a great deal of data and important collections that continue to be studied. A portion of the collections were taken to the Peabody Museum at Yale, where they remain today. Extensive analyses were done by Bingham and his colleagues and the project received a great deal of publicity. The National Geographic Society devoted the entire issue of their April 1913 magazine to Bingham's discovery. His story of trekking through the wilderness to discover a lost Inca city captured the public's

Left Located near the Main Plaza at Machu Picchu is the sacred Intihuatana, or 'hitching post of the Sun', which was used in Inca religious festivals. It is unique as the Spanish destroyed all other such stone structures as evidence of idolatry.

Above A panoramic view of Machu Picchu, with Mount Huayna Picchu towering in the background. The Inca builders constructed their remarkable buildings from stones cut to fit tightly together without mortar.

imagination. In one account he describes his first view of the site, 'We rounded a knoll and suddenly faced tier upon tier of Inca terraces rising like giant stairs. Each one, hundreds of feet long, was banked by massive stone walls up to ten feet high.'

Bingham abandoned archaeology after the Machu Picchu project, serving in the US military during World War I before entering into politics. He was elected as a member of the US Senate in 1924.

Royal estate

Although it was Bingham who put Machu Picchu on the map, most of his ideas have since been superseded by new information. We now know that Machu Picchu, far from being the last outpost of Inca royalty, had actually been abandoned by the time the Spanish arrived in Peru in 1532. Spanish colonial documents studied by the American archaeologist John Rowe and his students indicate that the site had in fact been built as a royal estate for the Inca ruler Pachacuti (AD 1438-71).

Machu Picchu was inhabited for most of the year by a relatively small group of retainers, with the palaces and other spectacular buildings reserved for seasonal use by the ruler and his entourage. The archaeological materials that Bingham recovered consist largely of everyday items used by those who lived at the site year-round, and not the fabulous luxury goods of the Inca elite. The materials found in the burials indicate that Machu Picchu's retainers came from throughout the Inca Empire, from the coast to the rainforest. Why the city was eventually abandoned, however, remains a mystery.

The site today

Bingham's theories about Machu Picchu may not have endured, but his legacy has, both in the US and in Peru. Archaeological exploration has continued at the site since Bingham's day and in 1983 it was listed as a World Heritage Site by UNESCO.

A recent exhibition entitled *Machu Picchu: Unveiling the mystery of the Inca*, organized by Yale University, toured the United States to great acclaim, sparking renewed interest and increased US tourism to Peru. The Peruvian government cooperated with Yale in the development of the exhibition, but it also requested that Yale return the Machu Picchu collections permanently to Peru.

Henri Breuil

(1877-1961)

Henri Edouard Prosper Breuil was one of the towering figures in the study of Old World prehistory during the first half of the 20th century, and was the pioneer of the study of Ice Age cave art. His views on Palaeolithic art were considered definitive by a whole generation of archaeologists.

Although the French archaeologist Henri Breuil trained as a priest in his youth, and remained one until his death, it was only a title – he was allowed to devote his whole existence to studying prehistory; he undertook virtually no religious duties, and made almost no contribution to the reconciliation of prehistory's findings with religious teachings.

Awakening

The son of a lawyer, Breuil was born and grew up in northern France, a place that infused him with an intense love of nature, especially of insects, and entomology remained a lifelong interest. An important early influence was his relative, the well-known geologist and archaeologist Geoffroy d'Ault du Mesnil, who showed Henri his collection of fossils and took him to the ancient sites of the Somme region. Here he met Louis Capitan, who introduced him to the study of prehistoric tools. Breuil also had the supreme good fortune, as a young man

with a talent for drawing animals, to make the acquaintance of Edouard Piette and Emile Cartailhac, two of France's greatest prehistorians at the turn of the century, when they needed help with the study and illustration of Palaeolithic portable and cave art.

Breuil was to go on to become the world's leading authority on Palaeolithic art until his death. He discovered many decorated caves or galleries himself, and copied their art – by his own reckoning he spent about 700 days of his life underground.

Although now seen as excessively subjective and incomplete, his tracings are nevertheless recognized as remarkable for their time. For some caves they constitute our only record of figures that have since faded or disappeared. Breuil concentrated not only on Palaeolithic art, but also on the megalithic art of France and (during World War I) the Iberian peninsula. In World War II he began a long campaign of copying rock art in parts of southern Africa.

Breuil's greatest contributions to tool typology were made in France, where he set out the first detailed description of the characteristic tools of each French Palaeolithic period, dividing the Magdalenian into six phases on the basis of changing tool types. This scheme was both durable and influential, but has now been replaced by a simpler and more flexible

Early/Middle/Upper Magdalenian. In the same way, Breuil conceived of two cycles in the development of Palaeolithic art, the 'Aurignaco-Perigordian' followed by the 'Solutreo-Magdalenian' – two essentially similar but independent cycles, each progressing from simple to complex forms in engraving, sculpture and painting. This system, however, was inconsistent and unsatisfactory, and was eventually replaced by the four 'styles' of André Leroi-Gourhan, themselves now in the course of abandonment.

Breuil saw Palaeolithic art primarily in terms of hunting magic, and he generally considered decorated caves to be accumulations of single figures, unlike Leroi-Gourhan who saw them as carefully planned compositions.

An irascible and egotistical man, Breuil nevertheless had a lasting influence on numerous devoted friends and pupils. So ingrained was his image as the 'Pope of Prehistory' that he was often thought virtually infallible. It is only in recent years that it has become possible in France openly to criticize and re-examine his work like that of any other scholar. His huge legacy of publications and tracings has been found to contain many errors, but equally an abundance of insights that are now supported by new finds.

Left A drawing of a bison from the cave of Altamira, in Spain. Breuil copied and published hundreds of examples of rock carvings and paintings from Europe and Africa.

Howard Carter

(1874-1939)

The discovery of the tomb of Tutankhamen in Egypt's Valley of the Kings in the 1920s is one of the great events in archaeology. The story behind this magnificent find by the English archaeologist Howard Carter continues to fire the imagination.

Howard Carter was born in London on 9 May 1874. Art was a major influence in his youth. His father, Samuel John Carter, was an artist known for his paintings of animal scenes. The young Howard's educational interests, however, led him down the route of history and archaeology. At the age of only 17, he started his Egyptological career, working as assistant to Percy Newberry in the rock-cut tombs of Beni Hasan and el-Bersha.

Early career

After a brief spell with Flinders Petrie at Amarna, Carter worked at the Delta site of Mendes. He then worked with Edouard Naville at the Deir el-Bahari mortuary temple, Thebes, until in 1899 he was offered a permanent position with the Egyptian Antiquities Service.

After five happy years working in Luxor, Carter was transferred to Saqqara. Here he became involved in a diplomatic incident. A party of drunken Frenchmen had attempted to force their way into the antiquities holdings, and Carter had allowed his workmen to defend themselves. Owing to the subsequent row, in which Carter sided with his local workers rather than with the Europeans, he resigned in October

1905 to become an artist and antiquities dealer. He would soon return to archaeology, however.

In 1909 Carter came under the patronage of Lord Carnarvon, who had made a visit to Egypt in 1905 and had been inspired to pursue some archaeological work there. Rather than permit Carnarvon himself to work unsupported, however, the Antiquities Service appointed Carter as the expert.

Three years' work in the Theban necropolis was followed by a brief excavation at Xois and a mission to Tell el-Balamun. The war years were spent working for the War Office in

Cairo, although Carter continued to undertake a series of small-scale digs at various sites.

Carter was convinced that the 18th Dynasty king Tutankhamen still lay in the Egyptian Valley of the Kings. However, as Theodore Davis had been granted sole permission to excavate in the Valley, Carter could only watch and wait. When, in 1914, Davis gave up his concession, the war prevented any new field work.

Royal tomb

In 1917 Carter began to clear the Valley. It was slow and expensive work, and Lord Carnarvon started to

Right A wall painting depicts Tutankhamen, riding on a chariot and firing arrows at the Nubian enemy. The vultures act as protective guardians over the king.

Above A throne found in the tomb of Tutankhamen, made from ebony and ivory with gilt features on the sides.

doubt the existence of the tomb. Eventually, it was agreed that there would be one last season. On 1 November 1922 workmen started to clear rubbish lying beneath the tomb of Ramesses VI. Three days later they discovered 16 steps leading to a blocked doorway. Carter rushed to the telegraph office to call his patron.

The drama of such moments was captured in Carter's journals, which he maintained throughout his work in the Valley. The following extract was written on Sunday, November 5: 'Though I was satisfied that I was on the verge of perhaps a magnificent find ... I was much puzzled by the smallness of the opening in comparison with those of other royal tombs in the valley. Its design was certainly of the XVIIIth Dyn. Could it be the tomb of a noble, buried there by royal consent? Or was it a royal cache? As far as my investigations had gone there was absolutely nothing to tell me. Had I known that by digging a few inches deeper I would have exposed seal impressions showing

Tut.ankh.Amen's insignia distinctly I would have fervently worked on and set my mind at rest ...'

Three weeks later work resumed. Soon it was possible to read the name of the tomb owner: 'Tutankhamen'. The doorway was dismantled, and the entrance corridor cleared.

By 26 November Carter had entered the antechamber, a storeroom packed with grave goods. A second chamber in the western wall, the 'annex', held more grave goods, while the northern wall included the sealed entrance to the burial chamber. It was to take the team seven long weeks to empty the antechamber. Each object had to be numbered, photographed, planned and drawn before it could be moved. On 17 February 1923 the wall sealing the burial chamber was demolished and an enormous gilt shrine was revealed. Inside was another gold shrine, then another, and another.

Later that month, however, Lord Carnarvon was bitten on the cheek by a mosquito. He sliced the scab off the bite while shaving, and started to feel unwell. Blood poisoning set in, and pneumonia followed. Lord Carnarvon died in Cairo on 5 April 1923.

Sarcophagus

On 3 January 1924, the doors of the innermost shrine were opened, revealing the sarcophagus. On 12 February, the cracked lid was hoisted

Below Howard Carter (left) stands holding a crowbar, having opened the doorway to the chamber of Tutankhamen's tomb. Arthur Mace of the Metropolitan Museum is on the right.

Above Wall paintings around Tutankhamen's sarcophagus. The Burial Chamber was the only part of the complex to contain wall paintings.

off the quartzite base. The next day the wives of the archaeologists were to be allowed a viewing of the coffin. The government objected, however. Carter was furious. Work stopped, and did not resume until early 1925.

Tutankhamen had been buried in three coffins – the outer pair made of gold-covered wood, and the inner coffin of solid gold. A gold mask had been placed over the mummy. Resin-based unguents had been poured over the dead king and they had hardened, gluing the king into his coffin. The golden mask, therefore, had to be removed using hot knives.

Carter spent a decade recording and preserving the tomb. Yet before he could complete the publication of his greatest work, he died in London on 2 March 1939.

King's burial

Tutankhamen's burial followed the funerary orthodoxy of ancient Egypt. Body fluids were purged, internal organs were removed and placed in canopic jars and the body was treated with the preservative natrum, the complete process lasting a required 70 days. The body was then wrapped in 13 layers of treated linen, into which were inserted 143 assorted amulets and charms. Tutankhamen's preparation was completed with a magnificent solid-gold death mask covering the head and shoulders. Objects found around the body included items of jewellery and flowers.

Right One of the two wooden and painted sentry statues posted in the antechamber at the sides of the walled door that led into the king's burial chamber.

G. Caton-Thompson

(1888-1985)

Gertrude Caton-Thompson is a towering figure in the history of African archaeology. Her work at Great Zimbabwe would cause an ideological storm in western academia, upsetting many of the racially motivated preconceptions about Africa prevalent at the time.

Born in London in 1888, Gertrude Caton-Thompson enjoyed a privileged upbringing and education. From Newnham College, Cambridge, she proceeded to the British School of Archaeology in Egypt, training under the eminent Egyptologist, Sir Flinders Petrie. With Elinor Gardner, she initiated the first archaeological survey of the northern Faiyum and served as a field director for the Royal Anthropological Institute. After further work on predynastic sites in Egypt, Caton-Thompson undertook work at the site of Great Zimbabwe, in modern Zimbabwe.

Great Zimbabwe

The extensive ruins in Africa had first been excavated by Theodore Bent in 1891, and then by R.N. Hall as part of the imperialist programme of Cecil John Rhodes. Hall, whose abilities as an excavator were questioned even in his own time, proposed that Great Zimbabwe was the site of the legendary goldfields of Ophir. He argued that Great Zimbabwe had been made by a highly civilized society that (almost by definition) could not be indigenous to Africa.

The British Association for the Advancement of Science sent David Randall-McIver to investigate. He concluded that the site was medieval in date and African in origin. When Caton-Thompson took over the excavations in 1929, she was able to demonstrate that Randall-McIver's ideas about Great Zimbabwe were valid. Working with two female assistants, she conclusively established the site's African origin.

Her findings challenged colonial prejudices about African inferiority and caused furore in an ongoing controversy about the intellectual capacity of African peoples and their place in colonial societies. Caton-Thompson, resolute in her findings and her scientific detachment, declared that she was quite 'unconcerned with speculations'.

Legacy

Caton-Thompson is remembered for her intrepid life and formidable personality as well as for her archaeological researches, which continued apace after her Zimbabwean work. In the early 1930s she conducted important excavations at the Egyptian site of Kharga Oasis, later working also in south-west Asia. In later life she was vice-president of the Royal Anthropological Institute, president of the British Prehistoric Society, held offices at the University of London and was a Fellow of Newnham College.

Her autobiography, *Mixed Memoirs*, was published in 1983 when she was in her mid-nineties. In it she describes herself as 'not easily alarmed'. Others have described her as 'fearless', 'fastidious' and possessed of 'extraordinary energy and powers of leadership'. She once listed her favourite recreation as 'idleness'. However, there is little evidence of her indulging in it. Gertrude Caton-Thompson retired in 1957 and died in Worcestershire in 1985.

Left The Great Enclosure, which was built in several stages, is the largest and most impressive structure at Great Zimbabwe.

Li Chi

(1896-1979)

Li Chi was one of the pioneers of modern Chinese archaeology. His familiarity with western methods of research gave him a fresh perspective on China's archaeological finds, and had a major impact on the quality of his field work, most famously at Anyang.

Regarded as the father of modern Chinese archaeology, Li Chi was born on 12 July 1896 in Zhongxiang, Hebei province. In the west he is best known for his excavation of the city of Anyang, Henan province, and his research on the so-called 'oracle bones'.

Although he had a Chinese education, Li Chi belonged to the first generation of Chinese archaeologists to be trained by leading scholars in universities and colleges in western Europe and the United States and, as such, was open to new methods of archaeological investigation. Li Chi studied anthropology and received a Ph.D. from Harvard in 1923.

In China Li Chi began working on Neolithic materials and soon became involved with the Academia Sinica's Institute of History and Philology, becoming its first director in 1928.

New research

At the beginning of the 20th century, field archaeology had been brought to China as a new western discipline. The Swedish geologist J.G. Andersson (1874-1960) discovered the first Neolithic site in China – the cave of Peking Man. Li Chi was the first Chinese archaeologist to apply western techniques on the first scientific excavation of Xiyincun, Anyang, carrying out field excavations in situ. A major focus of this new generation of Chinese archaeologists was to search for the origins of Chinese civilization and also to stop the looting of Chinese relics.

Old bones

In 1899 hundreds of bones inscribed with Chinese characters came to light in today's city of Anyang. They had been dug up by peasants and were being ground into medicine. It is said that in that year an official under the last of the Chinese dynasties, the Qing (1644-1911), fell ill and was prescribed 'dragon bones'. These bones, both tortoise shells and cattle shoulder blades, dated from about 3000 years earlier.

In 1928 the Academia Sinica decided to undertake excavations in Anyang at a site called Yin, the city that proved to be the last capital of the historical Shang Dynasty (1700-1027 BC) and the most important Bronze Age site in East Asia.

Between 1928 and 1937 a total of 15 seasons of excavations were carried out in Anyang under Li Chi's leadership. By 1937 archaeologists had excavated more than 100,000 objects, including thousands more inscribed bones, which they recognized as tools of divination. The ancient texts inscribed on the bones provide invaluable information about rulers, battles, folk religion and religious rites.

Excavations were halted by the outbreak of the Sino-Japanese war. Li Chi and his fellow research colleagues, together with their collection, were evacuated to western China. Publications and research continued and finally, in

1948, the Academia Sinica moved to Taiwan. Li Chi continued the work there and also trained young archaeologists, such as Kwang-Chih Chang (1931-2001), who finally brought the archaeology of China to the attention of the western world. In 1950 Li Chi became the head of anthropology and archaeology at the National University in Taipei and began directing publication of his remaining Anyang materials. He published a number of books, including *The Beginnings of Chinese Civilization* (1957) and *Anyang* (1977).

Li Chi died on 1 August 1979 in Taipei, Taiwan.

Above A food vessel cast in bronze with relief designs found at Anyang and dating from *c.*1300-1000 BC shows a high quality of workmanship.

Dorothy Garrod

(1892-1968)

An important figure in prehistoric studies, Dorothy Garrod conducted important excavations at the Palaeolithic caves of Mount Carmel in Israel, where she was able to identify the longest stratigraphic record in the region, spanning about 600,000 years of human activity.

The archaeologist and prehistorian Dorothy A.E. Garrod was the first woman to be appointed a professor at the University of Cambridge, holding the Disney Chair of Archaeology from 1939 to 1952. Garrod was the only daughter in a distinguished medical family, and the loss of her three brothers in World War I inspired her determination to achieve a life worthy of the family tradition, though in a different field. She was taught at Oxford by the prehistorian R.R. Marett and subsequently in France by Abbé Henri Breuil, who encouraged her research for her first book on the Upper Palaeolithic in Britain. Thereafter her work centred mainly on the Palaeolithic, with notable success.

Garrod owed her first major excavation (in 1926) to Breuil, who had identified the Devil's Tower site in Gibraltar. There she found a Middle Palaeolithic flint industry and the skull fragments of a Neanderthal child.

Rising reputation

The excavation and the publication of her findings established Garrod's place in Palaeolithic studies. Her lasting reputation was determined largely in Palestine during the years 1928-37, first by her excavation of Shukbah Cave in the Wadi en-Natuf. There she found human remains associated with a previously unknown Epipalaeolithic culture, which she named 'Natufian', whose people were apparently taking early steps towards agriculture. In a deeper level she recognized traces of Neanderthal occupation.

After a brief period in southern Kurdistan (where she identified further evidence of Middle and Upper Palaeolithic occupation), she returned to Palestine to begin the major work of her career in archaeology at the

Left Human remains at a Mount Carmel cave site. Garrod's excavations at Mount Carmel in the 1930s helped expand the anthropological picture of the Middle East.

Mount Carmel caves. In el Wad Cave she again found the Natufian culture, though in a later and richer phase than at Shukbah, with decorated burials and more complex lithic (stone) and bone industries.

Tabun Cave

In Tabun Cave, deepest of the group, the uppermost level corresponded to the lowest in el Wad, with a further seven levels descending to a pre-handaxe lithic industry. Garrod's skill in typological analysis enabled her to identify a cultural succession in the caves spanning some 600,000 years of human occupation. At different periods in history, Tabun and the nearby Skhul Cave 2 (which was excavated by her American colleague T.D. McCown) were occupied by two Palaeolithic human populations – Neanderthal and Anatomically Modern People – now known to have genetic differences.

Academic advance

Garrod's final report on the Mount Carmel excavation (*The Stone Age of Mount Carmel, vol.1*, 1937) established a new standard for its time, earning her a D.Sc. from Oxford University. When the Disney Chair at Cambridge became vacant, Garrod didn't think she stood much chance. She told a friend at the time, 'I shan't get it, but I thought I'd give the electors a run for their money'. Her election on the eve of World War II was an important landmark in higher education for women. In 1942 she was recruited to the RAF Medmenham Unit for Photographic Interpretation (staffed by several archaeological colleagues) for the duration of the war.

Returning to Cambridge, she worked to raise the status of archaeology as an academic subject in the university; it became part of the full Tripos and degree scheme in 1948.

Final work

Long vacations were devoted to excavation with French colleagues at the French sites of Fontéchevade and Angles-sur-l'Anglin. In 1952, four

years after women were admitted as full members of the university, she retired from Cambridge and settled permanently in France. In 1958 (aged 66) she resumed work in the Levant.

Garrod devoted this final phase of her working life to the eastern Mediterranean, where ancient caves and beaches preserved evidence that related Quaternary sea levels to the Ice Ages of Europe. Thus, when no absolute dating methods existed, their

Above As much as in Garrod's time, the Mount Carmel site is an enormous challenge to any archaeologist. The range is 26km (16 miles) long and reaches 7.2km (5 miles) wide.

respective prehistoric sequences could be correlated. However, the prolonged and difficult excavation, which ran from 1958 to 1963, was to take its toll on her health. She was awarded a CBE in 1965 three years before her death in Cambridge.

William Grimes

(1905-1988)

William Grimes devoted much of his career to the archaeology of both his native Wales and the city of London. His expertise in handling fragile sites saw him busily employed around the bomb-damaged capital during and following World War II. He is famous for his work on the London Mithraeum.

Born in Pembrokeshire, Wales, Grimes studied classics at the University of Wales in Cardiff and was employed in the National Museum of Wales. This brought him into contact with the prehistoric and Roman antiquities of Wales and his subsequent career reflects this dual interest. One of his first projects was the publication of material from the legionary workshops at Holt in north Wales, which had served the fortress at Deva (Chester). He worked on a number of prehistoric sites in Wales in the 1930s and in 1939 published a catalogue of prehistoric antiquities in the National Museum.

Grimes had developed an expertise in working on waterlogged sites that had preserved organic material. In 1938 he went to work as an archaeologist for the Ordnance Survey, which was responsible for mapping in the United Kingdom. It was in this capacity that he was invited to work with O.G.S. Crawford at the Sutton Hoo ship burial in Suffolk in 1939. Contemporary reports acknowledge his skill in extracting a range of delicate finds from the ground.

Wartime work

During World War II, Grimes was responsible for excavating many archaeological sites before their development as military locations, such as airfields. One of the more famous excavations conducted at this time was the Iron Age temple on the site of what is now Heathrow airport to the west of London.

In 1945 he was appointed director of the London Museum and was responsible for a number of rescue excavations in the city, which had been devastated by enemy bombing. In 1954 he famously excavated a Roman Mithraeum on a bomb site off Walbrook in central London. He succeeded in salvaging many of its finds, including marble statuary.

Grimes was appointed the director of the Institute of Archaeology in London in 1956 and subsequently served on many national bodies, where his archaeological expertise was much in demand.

Left Excavations at the Roman temple to the god Mithras in London. This photograph was taken on the site's public open day.

David Hogarth

(1862-1927)

Born in Lincolnshire into a clergy family, David George Hogarth went on to have a distinguished archaeological career. He conducted excavations at many locations in southern Europe and the Middle East, including Cyprus, Crete, Ephesus, Melos, Egypt and Syria.

As a young man Hogarth studied classics at Oxford and was the first student from that university to be admitted to the newly opened British School at Athens. One of his interests was in Greek inscriptions, which were seen as an important supplement to classical literary and historical texts. While at Athens he studied the inscriptions of Thessaloniki, then part of the Ottoman empire.

Ottoman Journey

In the late spring of 1887, Hogarth joined the archaeologist and biblical scholar William Mitchell Ramsay for a journey across Anatolia from Smyrna (Izmir) on the Aegean coast to Cilicia in the south-east. This was to be the first of a series of such travels in the Ottoman empire, and it included a survey of the upper Euphrates Valley. Hogarth's introduction to the world of archaeological excavation came on the island of Cyprus as part of the British project to record some of the classical sites there.

Hogarth's archaeological expertise took him to Egypt, initially to work on the Greek and Latin inscriptions found by Flinders Petrie. One of the projects in Egypt was a survey of Graeco-Roman Alexandria. In the mid-1890s he worked on a survey of the Faiyum in search of papyri that, it was hoped, would provide new examples of classical literature.

In 1897 Hogarth was appointed director of the British School at Athens. During this period there was

continuing work at the Bronze Age site of Phylakopi on Melos, and in 1899 Hogarth returned to the western Nile delta to work at the Greek trading station of Naukratis. With the removal of Crete from the control of the Ottoman empire, Hogarth turned his archaeological attention to the island, working on a number of sites including Knossos and Kato Zakro.

Hogarth next directed the British Museum excavations at Ephesus and in 1908 he returned to the Euphrates Valley to initiate work at Carchemish, where one of the excavators was T.E. Lawrence ('of Arabia'); the two men

Above Hogarth conducted an excavation of the Temple of Artemis at Ephesus between 1904 and 1905, publishing *The Archaic Artemisia of Ephesus* in 1908.

worked together during World War I when Hogarth ran the Arab Bureau in Cairo. In 1908 Hogarth was appointed Keeper of the Ashmolean Museum in Oxford. After war service in the eastern Mediterranean as part of the military intelligence community, Hogarth returned to Oxford where he developed his interest in the Hittites, publishing *Kings of the Hittites* in 1926. He remained keeper of the Ashmolean until his death in 1927.

Alfred Kidder

(1885-1963)

Alfred Vincent Kidder is still rightly regarded as one of the most important and influential American archaeologists, his reputation built on both his technical innovations in excavation and his contribution to theory, especially in the area of chronology building.

Alfred Kidder grew up in New England and originally wanted to become a physician. However, after entering Harvard he found himself uninspired by medical training and after taking a short course in anthropology became consumed by the subject, developing a particular interest in archaeology.

After working on sites in the American Southwest, mainly in Arizona and Utah, he changed his major and in 1914 received a Ph.D. in anthropology (concentrating on ceramics); he was only the sixth person in the United States to receive a doctorate that concentrated on this sub-discipline.

Chronologies

At the time American archaeology was still desperately trying to organize the burgeoning amount of data from excavations into some coherent system. Even in the Southwest, the technique of tree-ring dating was still in its infancy, and the most pressing concern there, as elsewhere on the continent, was to establish baseline chronologies. Kidder was well aware of

this when, in 1915, he initiated excavations at the Pecos Ruins in northern New Mexico, which at the time was the largest archaeological undertaking in the United States. This large complex prehistoric ruin was perfect for the application of stratigraphic excavations, whereby different levels in a variety of sites in a region could be identified by

Below The interior of a kiva (a dug-out used for religious ceremonies) at the Pecos ruins. Kidder was director of excavations at Pecos from 1915 to 1929.

Above An exterior view of a kiva at Pecos with the ruins of a mission in the background. Kidder's work helped the development of a cultural chronology of the American Southwest.

diagnosing their material culture. The temporal sequence could then be checked through excavation at other sites and then applied on a region-wide basis, so that a relative chronology between the sites could be established.

The sheer quantity of material coming out of Pecos, as well as from other archaeological excavations in the Southwest, led Kidder to convene the first Pecos Conference in 1927. The result was the so-called 'Pecos Classification', by which South-western prehistory was organized into a series of stages that quickly became time periods, each one recognizable by particular pottery styles and architectural forms. The selection of a relatively small number of temporally diagnostic artefacts per period is reminiscent of the geological process of identifying type fossils unique to a particular stratum. It is also similar to the 'chest-of-drawers' archaeology used for European prehistory. The Pecos Classification, with some modification, is still the primary time-space framework for the northern part of the American Southwest.

Theoretical attack

In 1929 Kidder took up a prestigious position with the Carnegie Institution in Washington, being appointed the director of the Division of Historical Research. Beginning in the 1930s, Kidder switched his practical interests to Central America and conducted excavations at Maya sites such as Chichén Itzá, among others. Kidder employed a team of inter-disciplinary scholars to try to portray as holistic a picture of the past as possible.

In 1950 Kidder retired from the Peabody Museum and Carnegie Institution, although he remained active in the field of archaeology up until his death in 1963. However, towards the end of his career Kidder became the target of an attack by one of archaeology's first 'angry young men', Walter Taylor. He argued that Kidder and his generation had held archaeology back for concentrating too much, in Taylor's view, on the construction of cultural history rather than investigating the processes by which cultures changed. In this, Taylor's critique presaged the revolution in archaeology of the 1960s called the 'New Archaeology', a revolution that explicitly advocated the scientific method to answer why and how cultures change through time and space. Kidder and others of his generation were, in Taylor's view, guilty of concentrating too much on the artefacts of the past, rather than trying to learn about the people who made and used them.

Despite this criticism, which stung Kidder personally, his place in the pantheon of American archaeologists is assured. The Society for American Archaeology, for instance, calls its most prestigious award after him.

Below An 800-year-old painted pottery bowl made by Anasazi Indians at Pecos, where Kidder excavated a large collection of pottery fragments.

Winifred Lamb

(1894-1963)

The classical archaeologist Winifred Lamb carried out pioneering excavations in Greece, the Aegean islands and Anatolia. She rose to become the honorary keeper of Greek Antiquities at the Fitzwilliam Museum, Cambridge.

Winifred Lamb was born in London, the only child of a colliery owner and Liberal Member of Parliament. She read classics at Newnham College, Cambridge. Upon completing her studies in 1917 she joined the Naval Intelligence Department (Room 40) at the Admiralty in London, where one of her colleagues was the Oxford archaeologist Sir John Beazley. It may have been at his prompting that she purchased Greek pottery from the Hope sale at Christies in 1917, which included part of the 18th-century collection formed by Sir William Hamilton. Lamb's first published article appeared in the *Journal of Hellenic Studies* in 1918.

Recognition

In 1919 Lamb was invited to become the honorary keeper of Greek and Roman Antiquities at the Fitzwilliam Museum, Cambridge. For nearly 40 years she fulfilled this role against a background of active field work in Greece and Turkey.

She was one of the first people to be admitted to the British School at Athens after World War I. One of her responsibilities was to work on the excavation of the Bronze Age palace at Mycenae under the direction of Alan Wace. Her interests in Greek prehistory are reflected by her creation of a prehistoric gallery back at the Fitzwilliam Museum.

Lamb became involved in pioneering excavations in Macedonia and she was keen to show a link between the Balkans and north-west Anatolia. She also worked with the British School's resumed excavations at the historical site of Sparta, where she published some of the small bronzes. Lamb had a strong interest in this category of antiquities and published one of the defining studies of Greek and Roman bronze statues.

The death of her father in 1925 gave Lamb the financial means to direct her own excavations and through the late 1920s and '30s she worked on a series of sites on the island of Lesbos, most notably Thermi. From Lesbos she looked to Anatolia and was one of the first women to excavate in the new republic of Turkey at the site of Kusura.

Lamb was badly injured in London during World War II when a German V2 rocket hit her lodgings, killing her housemates. Although this restricted her activities, she continued to travel in Turkey and was a moving force behind the creation of the British Institute of Archaeology in Ankara in 1948. She retired in 1958 and died of a stroke on 16 September 1963.

Left The theatre at Sparta, one of Winifred Lamb's excavation sites during the 1920s. She conducted her work at Sparta under the auspices of the British School at Athens. where she was admitted in 1920 and was in attendance there into the early 1930s. In 1931 she was given the title Honorary Student by the School.

Sir Max Mallowan

(1904-1978)

Better known to the wider world as the husband of the mystery writer Agatha Christie, Max Mallowan made lasting contributions to Mesopotamian archaeology. His work established the basic outline of the prehistoric and early historic cultures of northern Iraq and Syria.

Max Edgar Lucien Mallowan was born in London on 6 May 1904. The seeds of his interest in archaeology were planted at New College, Oxford, where he read classics. Following his graduation, Mallowan began an archaeological career at Ur, where he worked as an assistant to Leonard Woolley from 1925 to 1930.

Aged 26, he met Agatha Christie at Ur when she visited in 1930 and the two were married in Edinburgh six months later. Woolley, however, banned spouses from the field, and so Mallowan left Ur and worked with R. Campbell Thompson at Nineveh in 1931 and 1932.

At Nineveh Mallowan developed a stratigraphic sequence for that long-occupied site; the sequence survives today in the name Ninevite 5, in reference to an early 3rd-millennium BC pottery style.

Major projects

Mallowan launched his first independent project in 1933, at Arpachiyah in northern Iraq. He would spend the best part of a year at the site, and during his excavations there he exposed remains of Halaf (6th millennium BC) and of Ubaid (5th millennium BC) occupations. Arpachiyah remains an important reference site for the Halaf culture, known for its elaborately painted pottery and circular *tholos* houses.

Mallowan then moved his field work to Syria during the remainder of the 1930s. At Chagar Bazar he found a

Below A Middle Eastern sculpture from the 3rd millennium BC depicts a bull's body with a human head. Mallowan found many such zoomorphic images during his work in Iraq and Syria. Tragically, many of the Nimrud ivories discovered under Mallowan's direction were looted or damaged in Baghdad during the fighting of 2003.

cultural sequence beginning with Halaf materials and continuing into the 2nd millennium BC. At Tell Brak he uncovered the Uruk-period Eye Temple (*c.* 3500-3100 BC), so named for the many small stone idols with prominent eyes found there, and a palace belonging to the Akkadian king Naram Sin (2213-2176 BC). In the Balikh Valley he undertook a survey and soundings at several sites.

Knighthood

In 1949, having been recently named director of the British School of Archaeology, Baghdad (a position he kept until 1961), Mallowan resumed the long-interrupted excavations at

Nimrud, which he continued until 1957. The project focused on the domestic quarters and administrative wing of the North-west Palace, and also explored the remains of Fort Shalmaneser, along with other palaces, temples and private houses near the city wall. The most spectacular result was the discovery of the Nimrud ivories.

Mallowan garnered many academic positions during his career, including president of the British Institute of Persian Studies between 1961 and 1978, and received a knighthood in 1968. He wrote his autobiography *Mallowan's Memoirs* in 1977, a year before his death.

Sir John Marshall

(1876-1958)

John Marshall's defining work was at Taxila in India, to which he committed over 20 years of research and investigation. Marshall also directed excavations at Mohenjo-Daro, work that would alter the historical understanding of the Indian subcontinent.

John Hubert Marshall was born on 19 March 1876 in Chester. Having attended Dulwich College as a young man, he then proceeded to King's College, Cambridge, where he undertook a Classical Tripos between 1898 and 1900.

Early work

Marshall gainied invaluable experience of excavation and archaeological exploration at the British School in Athens, where many of Britain's foremost archaeologists would cut their teeth. In 1902 he was appointed Director-General of Archaeology in India, a post that had been in abeyance for more than a decade. India's long and varied history had left a wealth of art and architecture whose preservation had been sadly neglected, and little of its rich prehistory had been investigated. Marshall devised and initiated appropriate conservation measures for known monuments and began a programme of excavations.

Among his main foci were the Early Historic cities and Buddhist monuments located by Sir Alexander Cunningham, who had retired as director-general in 1885 after decades of exploring sites known from early Buddhist literature.

Marshall's principal excavation, begun in 1913 and continued until 1936, was at Taxila, a long-lived

Above Here is the famous 'Priest King' of Mohenjo-Daro, discovered by Marshall during his work there in the 1920s. Note the ornamentation around the forehead and the broad trefoil sash.

trading, political and cultural centre, but he and his officers also investigated other Early Historic cities, including the site of Pataliputra. Equally important was the clearance, survey, excavation and restoration of Buddhist monasteries and stupas (relic mounds). Between 1912 and 1919 Marshall also worked at Sanchi, where the Mauryan emperor Ashoka had built a stupa to house relics of the Buddha. This had been enlarged and several others were constructed by later kings, along with monasteries. Marshall concentrated

Left Mohenjo-Daro has produced some of the finest archaeological finds in the Indian sub-continent, and at one time had an estimated 35,000 occupants.

on the Great Stupa, revealing its magnificent gateways, lavishly decorated with reliefs depicting scenes from the Buddha's life, as well as figures from folk tradition.

A few prehistoric Indian sites were known, but the Early Historic cities that emerged in the mid-1st millennium BC were thought to have been the first flowering of Indian civilization. This picture was changed dramatically in 1922, when investigations by Archaeological Survey officers at Harappa and Mohenjo-Daro in the Indus valley unexpectedly revealed the remains of two great cities with distinctive and previously unknown material that was clearly considerably older than the Early Historic period.

Marshall publicly announced their discovery in 1924; Mesopotamian scholars were immediately able to demonstrate that the Indus Civilization, as it was now called, had been contemporary with Sumer, the first civilization in the Near East.

Mohenjo-Daro

Marshall took personal control at Mohenjo-Daro for the major excavation season of 1925-6, assisted by senior staff and with more than a thousand labourers.

The excavations revealed a huge and well-planned city with brick drains and many public wells. Often the houses had bathrooms and private wells. The city was divided into two parts — the residential Lower Town, and a higher Citadel Mound, soon identified as the locus of important public buildings. These included the Great Bath, a large rectangular tank of baked brick made watertight with bitumen, probably for ritual bathing.

One part of the Lower Town yielded a quantity of jewellery, including a fine necklace of extremely long

Right The Great Stupa at Sanchi (the dome rising in the background) was the focus of one of Marshall's great studies. An elegantly carved gateway (torana) depicts scenes of Buddhist worship.

carnelian beads. Etched carnelian beads were found widely within the city, as were pottery vessels decorated with fishscale, geometric and animal designs. There were many steatite seals also bearing animal designs, particularly the unicorn, along with a few signs in what was now identified as the Indus script. In one building was discovered a rare piece of sculpture, depicting the head and upper torso of a bearded man wearing a garment decorated with trefoils — the now-famous 'Priest-king'.

After one season Marshall returned to his work at Taxila, but excavations continued at Mohenjo-Daro until 1931. Outstanding finds included the lively bronze statuette, known as the 'dancing-girl', and the so-called 'Proto-Shiva' seal, which bears a design showing a three-faced horned deity surrounded by wild animals.

Marshall officially retired as director-general in 1928, but continued to work until 1934 when he returned to England. There he

Above A steatite seal from Mohenjo-Daro, depicting an elephant and assorted monograms and dating from around 2500 BC.

worked on the mammoth report on his excavations at Taxila, which finally emerged in 1951.

The list of publications he left at the time of his death on 17 August 1958 included *The Monuments of Sanchi* (reprinted 1983), a large three-volume work which he co-authored with Alfred Foucher.

Pierre Montet

(1885-1966)

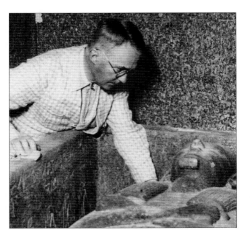

Pierre Montet is most closely associated with the one-time royal capital, Tanis, in the northern Nile Delta. Here, just before and after World War II, he discovered a series of magnificent burials dating from the 21st and 22nd Dynasties in the 11th-8th centuries BC.

Born at Villefranche-sur-Saône in the Beaujolais region of central France, Montet first studied Egyptology at the University of Lyon, where he was taught by Victor Lore, a former head of the Egyptian Antiquities Service. He then moved to the French Institute of Eastern Archaeology in Cairo until the outbreak of World War I.

Royal tombs

From 1921 to 1924 Montet excavated at the Lebanese site of Byblos, where he discovered a temple and a series of tombs belonging to local rulers. This early work sparked a lifelong interest in the connections between Egypt and her eastern neighbours. In 1929 he began work in the Nile Delta at Tanis, the Egyptian capital during the 21st and 22nd Dynasties. It was also the favoured burial place of the monarchs of these dynasties, who abandoned the royal necropolis in the Valley of the Kings in favour of the better-guarded precincts of the temples there. The French archaeologist Auguste Mariette carried out excavations at the great Amen temple of Tanis in 1859, discovering a series of 12th-Dynasty royal sculptures; now Montet cleared the temple area, uncovering yet more royal statuary.

His greatest finds, however, came from a temple dedicated to the goddess Mut (known elsewhere in the eastern Mediterranean as Anta or Astarte), where in February 1939 he discovered a multi-chambered royal tomb (labelled Tomb I) lying beneath ruined Ptolemaic buildings. Buried there were King Osorkon II and his son Prince Hornakht.

In a neighbouring tomb (Tomb III), which he entered in March 1939, he found the disturbed burial chamber of Psusennes I and the mummies of Sheshonq II and Siamun, along with the undisturbed chambers of Psusennes II and Amenemope (who had usurped a chamber originally prepared for Queen Mutnodjmet).

The outbreak of World War II brought the work at Tanis to a halt, but as soon as peace returned Montet was back. In February 1946 he discovered the burial chamber of General Wendjebauendjedet, also in Tomb III. Today, the contents of these magnificent burials are displayed in Cairo Museum.

Montet was Professor of Egyptology at the University of Strasbourg (1919-48), then at the Collège de France, Paris. He published many books and articles, including *La Nécropole Royale de Tanis* (1958), *Everyday Life in the Days of Ramesses the Great* (1958) and *Eternal Egypt* (1964). He also founded the journal *Kêmi*. He died in Paris on 19 June 1966.

Left An overview of the arrowhead fortification wall at Byblos. Systematic excavations of the ancient Phoenician city did not begin until the 1920s.

André Parrot

(1901-1980)

André Parrot helped shape our cultural and historical understanding of the Middle East. His archaeological career stretched from the 1920s to the 1970s, and he is best known for his 40-year directorship of the excavations at Mari in Syria.

Parrot was born on 15 February 1901, the son of a minister, Charles Parrot. Like his father, Parrot seemed destined for a religious career, studying Protestant theology at the Sorbonne. However, a series of art history courses at the École du Louvre, then a year of antiquity sciences at the École Biblique et Archéologique Française in Jerusalem, expanded his interests to include archaeology, particularly that of the Near East.

Between 1926 and 1933 Parrot undertook numerous excavations, first at Nerab in northern Syria then Baalbek in the Lebanon, before moving to the Mesopotamian sites of Telloh (originally Girsu, capital of Lagash state) and Tell Senkere (Larsa). He directed excavations at Telloh and Tell Senkere from 1961 to 1967.

Life achievement

In 1933 Parrot began excavations at Tell Hariri in Syria, formerly ancient Mari. He was director of work there until 1972, during which time the site yielded constant riches, including over 20,000 cuneiform clay tablets and the Old Babylonian palace of Zimri-Lim (1782-1759 BC). Parrot commented that 'each time a vertical probe was commenced in order to trace the site's history down to virgin soil, such important discoveries were made that horizontal digging had to be resumed'.

Parrot's work in the Middle East ran alongside professional advancement in France. He became the Inspecteur Géneral des Musées in France in 1965, and the Louvre's director between 1968 and 1972. He held numerous other institutional and honorary academic posts. Parrot was also a prolific author, his works including *Sumer* (1960), *Assur* (1961) and *L'aventure archéologique* (1979). Many of his writings explored the relationship

Above A haunting figure from the Mari Temple of Ishtar, created from alabaster, gypsum and lapis lazuli.

between biblical scripture and archaeology, Parrot believing that the latter threw a 'powerful light ... upon the religion and beliefs of a people in search of supernatural forces'.

Right Parrot remains the central figure behind the excavations at Mari, to which he dedicated much of his working life. He probed its history back to its foundations in around 2900 BC.

Sir Flinders Petrie

(1853-1942)

The British Egyptologist Flinders Petrie transformed both our knowledge of ancient Egypt and the techniques of field archaeology. In particular, he developed sequence dating, a method of reconstructing the histories of ancient cultures on the basis of their pottery and other remains.

Surveying was in the blood for Flinders Petrie. His father was an engineer and surveyor, and his grandfather was the navigator Matthew Flinders, who first charted large parts of the coast of Australia. Flinders Petrie was still only in his late teens when he started recording the prehistoric monuments of southern England. Later, with his father's assistance, he made the most accurate survey of Stonehenge at that time.

The Great Pyramid

In 1880, aged 26, he made his first trip to Egypt to survey the Great Pyramid at Giza. At the time, many believed that the pyramid had been built using a divinely inspired 'pyramid inch' as the basic unit of measurement – some even thought this was related to the cubit used to build Noah's Ark and the Tabernacle of Moses. Petrie wanted to find out the truth. Employing just one workman,

he spent two seasons on the survey and structural examination. The end result, so accurate that Petrie's survey is still used today, showed that the 'pyramid inch' theory was false.

In 1883 he started working for the newly founded Egypt Exploration Fund, with excavations at Tanis (modern San el-Hagar) in the Nile

Below A view of the Great Pyramid, one of the Seven Wonders of the Ancient World.

Delta. This was followed by a season at the Greek trading centre Naucratis (el Nibeira). Later, with the support of two wealthy private backers – the Manchester businessman Jesse Haworth and the collector Martyn Kennard – he moved to Hawara in the Faiyum region, south-west of Cairo. Here, on the north side of the Middle Kingdom pyramid of Amenemhat III, he found a large Roman cemetery, which yielded a series of mummies with beautifully painted wood-panel faces. Next, he moved to Illahun (Lahun), also in the Faiyum region, where he excavated some 1800 rooms in a village that had been built for pyramid construction workers.

After a brief interlude working in Palestine, Petrie returned to Egypt, working first at the pyramid cemetery of Meidum, then at Akhetaten (modern Amarna). In Akhetaten he was denied access to the royal tombs, so he excavated in the central city instead, uncovering a beautiful painted gypsum pavement in the Great Palace.

Devising sequence dating

In April 1892 Petrie was appointed Professor of Egyptology at University College, London. From then on, he taught for half the year and spent the winter months in Egypt.

At Koptos (ancient Gebtu, modern Quft), Petrie discovered a series of statues, including three prehistoric colossal sculptures representing the fertility god Min. At Tûkh, close to the southern town of Nagada, he investigated a curious cemetery housing many hundreds of prehistoric graves – the remains of the peoples who had lived in the Nile valley before Egypt became one unified country. There were no texts with these graves, and so Petrie had to devise a new way of dating them, which came to be called sequence dating. This involved identifying the different types of pottery associated with the different burials, and using these to arrange the burials into successive chronological phases.

Excavations at Luxor, Qurna, Deshasha and Dendera followed. Petrie then moved to Abydos, where he was principally interested in the tombs of the 1st and 2nd Dynasty kings. He re-investigated 13 royal tombs, which allowed him to join his prehistoric Nagada grave sequence to the beginning of Egyptian history. He continued his field work at Giza, where he discovered 2nd Dynasty tombs which confirmed that Giza had been used as a cemetery long before Khufu built his Great Pyramid. In a cemetery at another site, Tarkhan, he found amazing quantities of textiles.

Then, in 1914, the Egyptian government imposed a change in archaeological protocol. All future excavations were to be under strict state control.

Above The Sphinx at Memphis excavated by Petrie in 1912. The Sphinx, 8m (26ft) long, is carved from a single piece of alabaster.

The old practice of dividing finds on a more or less 50:50 basis between the excavator and the Egyptian state was abolished; from this point on, all discoveries would automatically remain in Egypt unless the authorities chose to make an exception. These new regulations caused problems for Egyptologists like Petrie, whose private backers expected to receive some material reward for their funding. As a result, Petrie left Egypt after World War I to work in Palestine instead. He retired from University College, London, in 1933 and died in Jerusalem on 29 July 1942, at the age of 89.

Julio C. Tello

(1880-1947)

The Peruvian Julio C. Tello was one of those rare archaeologists whose work shaped the way an entire nation perceived itself. He expanded Peru's understanding of its pre-Columbian past, and also invested much of his time and effort training future generations of archaeologists.

Julio C. Tello is considered the Father of Peruvian Archaeology by most Peruvians. His work was central to establishing the importance of the early civilizations of Peru among academics, the public and, significantly, among Peru's political class. His work synthesizing and summarizing the sequence of ancient civilizations of the Andes, as well as at specific sites such as the famous Chavín de Huantar, inspired a generation of young archaeologists.

Tello was to become the first academically trained Peruvian archaeologist. His career included service as the director of the National Museum, as a professor at Peru's most important universities and even in the Peruvian congress. He established major museum collections, trained dozens of Peruvian archaeologists and promulgated laws to protect Peru's archaeological sites and resources. He also helped establish Peru's pre-Columbian past as an important part of her history.

Below The ruins of a wall at the site of Chavín de Huantar, Peru.

Right A carved stone nail head (Cabezas Clavas) at Chavín de Huantar.

Early promise

Tello was born and raised in the highlands of Huarochiri, outside Lima. He went to Peru's capital to study, working for the famous Peruvian intellectual Ricardo Palma and becoming interested in archaeology. He studied medicine, graduating from San Marcos University with a thesis on syphilis in ancient Peru in 1908. He then earned a scholarship to Harvard, where he did his post-graduate studies. During this time he worked with the famous physical anthropologist Ales Hrdlicka. Upon his return from the United States, Tello focused his work largely on pre-Inca civilizations in Peru. His work at Chavín de Huantar and other sites was extremely influential.

Scientific archaeology was in its infancy at the beginning of Tello's career, and many scholars at the time believed that civilization had emerged in only a few places, then spreading, or diffusing, to far-reaching areas. Peru was viewed, by the German scholar Max Uhle among others, as part of a larger American civilization that had its roots in Central America rather than locally. Tello disputed this idea, and much of his work was focused on establishing the local origins of Andean civilization. His work at Chavín de Huantar was particularly important.

Challenging ideas

Radiocarbon dating and other chronometric methods had yet to be invented, and stylistic analysis and stratigraphy were the main methods of assigning relative dates to, and establishing the relationships in time and space among, archaeological cultures and materials. Tello argued that Chavín greatly pre-dated Inca and other later Andean civilizations, and that it formed the original, or matrix, civilization of the Andes. More recent work has demonstrated that the origins of Peruvian civilization

pre-date even Chavín. The Chavín were, however, one of the first groups whose style spread widely across the Andean region. The influence of the Chavín style can be seen in architecture, pottery and other objects made throughout a wide area of Peru about 2500 years ago.

Archaeologists now believe that Chavín de Huantar was a major political and religious centre with trading relationships that extended from Peru's desert coast to the jungle. Tello published widely, writing books and newspaper articles during his lifetime, and he left reams of unpublished notes (some have been published posthumously).

While many of his ideas have been updated or modified by more recent studies, new techniques and more detailed analysis, Tello's influence is still felt today in several ways. First, Tello was correct in his assertions that Peruvian civilization developed locally, and we now know that the cultural sequence of the Andes extends back well over 12,000 years. Second, Chavín de Huantar was, as Tello believed, one of the most important early sites in the Andes, although it was neither the first nor the only early centre of civilization. Finally, Tello and some of his contemporaries shifted the perspective of Peru's intellectual and

political communities concerning the nature of Peruvian history and the importance of the pre-Columbian past and the indigenous civilizations. Peru's ancient civilizations and local traditions are now viewed by many educated Peruvians as a significant part of their country's past, and as something to be claimed as heritage by all Peruvians.

Below A relief sculpture covers the ruins of a monolith at Chavín de Huantar, Peru. Tello's work revealed much about the sophistication of early Andean culture.

MODERN ARCHAEOLOGISTS

With a few exceptions such as Mary Leakey, it is probably fair to say that the archaeologists of the mid- to late-20th century have not become household names. The increasingly scientific and academic nature of the subject has generally brought relative anonymity, except for those who feature on television. Nevertheless, the quality of the work carried out has constantly improved in tandem with the battery of new techniques available for dating, analysis, excavation and survey. The great archaeologists of the 20th century, including Ignacio Bernal, Rhys Jones, Kathleen Kenyon, Michael Ventris and others featured here, have dramatically deepened our understanding of human civilization. The scope of subject areas and locations has been incredibly diverse, ranging from the decipherment of Linear B to excavations at the ancient Zapotec capital of Monte Albán (facing page), and from new interpretations of Palaeolithic art to pioneering studies in Aboriginal Australia.

Meave Leakey Continuing the Leakey family tradition, her work has helped to redefine our understanding of human evolution.

Maria Reiche Her life's work was devoted to the Nasca lines etched into the face of the Peruvian desert.

Spyridon Marinatos He excavated an ancient city preserved under volcanic rock on the island of Thera (Santorini).

Manolis Andronikos

(1919-1992)

The discovery of rich royal tombs from the 4th century BC at Vergina in Greece — which Andronikos identified with the Macedonian king Philip II, father of Alexander the Great — marked the pinnacle of a long, prestigious career in archaeology.

Above A small ivory head of a bearded man, which Andronikos identified with Philip II, was excavated from Tomb II.

Manolis Andronikos was born in Prousa (the Turkish city of Brusa) on 23 October 1919, the son of Greek parents who had settled in Salonica (or Thessaloniki) after World War I.

At the age of 17 he joined the excavations of the Macedonian royal palace at Vergina, which were being undertaken by K.A. Rhomaios. These uncovered an impressive series of sumptuous dining rooms that gave views over the great western plain of Macedonia. Andronikos's career was interrupted by the German occupation of Greece during World War II. After serving with the Greek forces in the Middle East, he later resumed his studies at the Aristotelian University of Thessaloniki, receiving his doctorate in 1952. From there he went to Oxford where he worked with Sir John Beazley, whose expertise lay in the field of Greek, and especially Athenian, figure-decorated pottery.

Vergina

From Oxford Andronikos returned to Thessaloniki, first as a lecturer and then as professor of archaeology. He next worked on a series of excavations in Macedonia, eventually returning to the royal palace at Vergina in 1962, where his interest in archaeology had begun. He also turned his attention to the Iron Age burials around Vergina, and in particular to the Great Mound that lay at the heart of an extensive mound cemetery around the modern town. Excavations were initiated in 1976 and Andronikos uncovered two burials, one of which remained intact.

Tomb II was particularly rich, with a series of silver drinking vessels and jugs, an ivory-inlaid couch, elaborate armour and a stone sarcophagus, which held a solid gold burial chest, or larnax. The British scholar Nicholas Hammond had proposed that Vergina was the site of the ancient Macedonian capital of Aegae, which led Andronikos to conclude that he had opened the grave of one of the members of the Macedonian royal family. He also believed that the plate and pottery from the tomb should be dated to the third quarter of the 4th century BC. On this evidence he concluded that this must be the burial of Philip II of Macedonia, who had been assassinated in the theatre at Aegae.

The cremated remains found in the larnax in Tomb II were those of a middle-aged man. A team of professional forensic archaeologists from the University of Manchester have attempted a reconstruction based on known images of Philip II.

Left The site of the Macedonian Royal Palace at Vergina. In 1993 an underground building was constructed to enclose and protect the royal tombs. The treasures found in the tombs have been on display since 1997.

Tomb III contained a beautiful silver hydria (a Greek water jar) decorated with a gold wreath. This had been used as the container for the cremated remains of an individual who was aged about 14. A likely candidate is Alexander IV, who was murdered around the year 309 BC.

Disputed finds

Scholars have now started to question the date of Tomb II and therefore the identification with Philip II. The Attic black-glossed 'saltcellars' may be as late as the early 3rd century BC, and the barrel-vaulted style of the tomb may have been introduced to Macedonia after the eastern conquests of Philip's son, Alexander the Great. The Lion Hunt frieze that decorated

the front of Tomb II also seems more in keeping with the iconography of Alexander and his successors.

Recent re-examination of all the skeletal evidence from the tomb has suggested that the body had been cremated some time after the person had died, which makes it unlikely to be that of Philip II. Moreover, questions have been raised about the identification of damage to one of the

eyes that had convinced many that this was indeed Philip, who was known to have been blinded in one eye by an arrow injury. It has now been proposed that Philip II was, in fact, buried in (the robbed) Tomb I adjacent to a hero shrine that is likely to have been associated with a religious cult linked to Philip II.

Andronikos continued his work at Vergina, and subsequently revealed many more royal tombs. He wrote up his findings in *The Royal Graves at Vergina* (1978) and *Vergina: The Royal Tombs and the Ancient City* (1984). He received the Order of the Phoenix from the Greek government, Greece's highest civilian honour, just prior to his death on 30 March 1992.

Left The exquisite burial chest (larnax) that Andronikos found in Tomb II at Vergina. The solid gold chest, weighing 11kg (24lb), bears the distinctive Macedonian starburst on its lid.

Ignacio Bernal
(1910-1992)

One of the giants of Mexican archaeology, Ignacio Bernal devoted his long and distinguished career to unravelling the archaeological history of the Oaxaca valley of southern Mexico, and in particular the Zapotec capital of Monte Albán.

Although he was born into a distinguished family of historians, Bernal did not turn to archaeology until he was in his early thirties, when he began working with the great archaeologist Alfonso Caso at Monte Albán. Thus began a close collaboration with Caso and a life-long commitment to the archaeology of Oaxaca. Very little was known about the Zapotecs prior to Caso and Bernal's work, but based on their extensive archaeological explorations, and those of subsequent scholars, Oaxaca is now among the best-known regions of Mesoamerica.

Below A spectacular view across the ruins at Monte Albán. By AD 300 the population of the city numbered around 50,000.

Bernal received his PhD in 1950 from the National Autonomous University of Mexico (UNAM) and enjoyed a diverse career that included both administrative posts directing the National Institute of Anthropology and History (1968-71) and the National Museum of Anthropology (1962-68 and 1970-77). He served as a cultural attaché in Paris, and as president of the Society for American Archaeology (1968-69). In addition to his active service, he was a charismatic instructor both at the UNAM (1948-76) and at Mexico City College (1951-59).

Monte Albán

Bernal worked at Monte Albán from 1942 to 1944 and again between 1946 and 1953. His initial research

Above The oldest carved stones at the site are the so-called *danzantes* (dancers), depicting the contorted figures of slain captives. These slabs were displayed on façades and bear some of the earliest hieroglyphs known in Mesoamerica.

considered the Formative era of Monte Albán (500 BC to AD 200), while his dissertation was based on the late Classic period (AD 500-800), spanning the rise and decline of the great city.

He also branched out from Monte Albán to explore other areas both within the valley of Oaxaca and in the mountainous Mixteca region to the west. His projects at Coixtlahuaca and Tamazulápan were among the first scientific investigations of the Mixtecs, a cultural group of great interest to his colleague Caso.

Bernal also led a long-term project at Yagul (1954-62), where a Postclassic palace complex revealed the final phase of pre-Hispanic Oaxaca. The interaction of Mixtec peoples in the Zapotec region of Oaxaca was documented in colonial histories, and Bernal sought to apply archaeological rigour to test the chronicles. Between 1966 and 1972,

Bernal returned to his interest in Formative Oaxaca, directing an extensive project at the site of Dainzu, contemporary with the founding of Monte Albán, where carved stones depict the pre-Columbian ballgame.

Lifetime's work

Bernal's prolific publication record was documented on his 80th birthday, when it tallied 267 books and articles. Notable contributions include a book on the funerary urns of Oaxaca (with A. Caso), *Mexico Before Cortes* (1975; originally published in Spanish in 1959), an exhaustive bibliography of Mesoamerican archaeology and ethnography with 30,000 entries, a comprehensive volume on the ceramics of Monte Albán (with A. Caso and J. Acosta), which is popularly referred to as the 'blue bible', and *A History of Mexican Archaeology* published in 1980.

As is demonstrated by the tremendous scope of Bernal's publications, as well as his active service to Mexican archaeology and to

training archaeology students, Bernal was passionate about his craft and tirelessly committed to sharing his passion with academic and popular audiences alike. France awarded him the Légion d'Honneur in 1964 and Britain the Royal Order of Victoria in 1975. Similar honours were also

Above The ballcourt at Monte Albán. There are no stone rings and the court is shaped like a capital 'I'. Some experts think that the sloping walls were used in the game, not for spectators.

bestowed on him by countries including Germany, Italy, Belgium, Denmark and the Netherlands.

Monte Albán

The capital of the Zapotec empire between 500 BC and AD 800, Monte Albán (which means 'white mountain' in Spanish) was arguably the first urban centre in Mesoamerica. Located on a series of ridges, the city looms 300m (1000ft) above the valley of Oaxaca. Its acropolis was artificially modified into an enormous plaza surrounded by pyramids and civic-ceremonial buildings. Hieroglyphic texts, many of which remain undeciphered, represent the earliest known writing system in the Americas, and low-relief carvings embedded in the architectural façades depict sacrificial victims and imperial conquest.

While much of the initial reconstruction was directed by Caso and Bernal, research has continued through intensive survey of the 2000+ residential terraces, excavations of elite and commoner residences, and archaeo-astronomical interpretations of the enigmatic Building J. Together with the settlement-pattern surveys of the valley surrounding the city and investigations at many of the subordinate sites in the region, Oaxaca is one of the best-known regions for interpreting pre-Columbian Mesoamerica.

Alfonso Caso

(1896-1970)

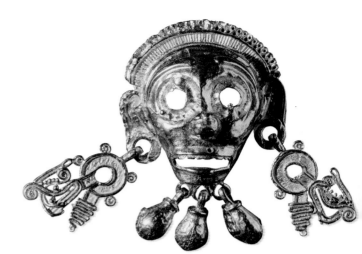

The Mexican archaeologist Alfonso Caso made important contributions to pre-Columbian studies in Mexico. His most celebrated discovery was Tomb VII at Monte Albán, which presented components of both Zapotec and Mixtec cultures.

Born in Mexico City in 1896, Alfonso Caso was one of the foremost Mexican archaeologists of the 20th century. He shaped the direction of the Mexican archaeological and anthropological institutions, while also making numerous major contributions to the interpretation of the pre-Columbian cultures of Mesoamerica. Caso's early training

Below An impressive view across the Grand Plaza at Monte Albán. Building J, in the foreground, may have been an observatory.

was as a lawyer, but early on his imagination was captured by the ancient cultures of his country and he began studying at the School of Advanced Studies under renowned scholars, such as Eduard Seler, Hermann Beyer and Manuel Gamio. He was later awarded an honorary doctorate from the National Autonomous University of Mexico.

Over the course of his career, Caso founded many of the cornerstones of Mexican archaeology, including the *Revista Mexicana de Estudios*

Above A gold bead, beautifully carved in the shape of a mask, shows the sophistication of pre-Columbian metalworking.

Antropológicos (*Mexican Journal of Anthropological Studies*), the National Institute of Anthropology and History, the National School of Anthropology and History and the National Indigenous Institute. Particularly in the second half of his career, he was deeply committed to the development of the discipline of anthropological archaeology.

Oaxaca

Caso is best known for his archaeological investigations in central Mexico, particularly in the state of Oaxaca. His long-term excavation at Monte Albán, the capital of the Zapotec civilization, added important breadth to a pre-Columbian history dominated at the time by Maya and Aztec cultures.

In addition to clearing and restoring numerous monumental structures on the ceremonial acropolis, Caso and his team also explored 180 tombs in elite residential compounds. The most famous of these was Tomb VII, where over 500 elaborately worked precious objects of gold, silver, jade, turquoise, alabaster and shell were found in association with a shrine to an earth/fertility goddess. Prominent among the grave offerings were carved weaving battens, inscribed with texts using the Mixtec hieroglyphic writing. Spurred on by these discoveries, Caso gained further

Above An ornate gold pendant excavated from Tomb VII at Monte Albán. This and other treasures from the tomb are now kept in the Oaxaca regional museum.

renown by making significant strides in the practical decipherment of this complex writing system.

Above A section of a pre-Columbian codex, named the Codex Zouche-Nuttall and now in the British Library in London. It is one of three codices that record the genealogies, alliances and conquests of several 11th- and 12th-century rulers of a small Mixtec city-state in Oaxaca.

Legacy

The inter-relationship of archaeology and epigraphy was a trademark focus of Caso, who also published works on Aztec and Tarrascan calendar systems. His several books on the Aztecs, notably *People of the Sun* (1958), remain among the most important treatments of the subject. His other publications include *Thirteen Masterpieces of Mexican Archaeology* (1938).

A true 'Renaissance-style' scholar, Caso's interests were diverse and his approach to research rigorous. In recognition of his profound influence on Mexican archaeology, he was buried in 1970 in the Rotunda of Illustrious Men in Mexico City.

Rhys Jones

(1941-2001)

Welsh-born archaeologist Rhys Jones was a true pioneer of modern Australian archaeology. Through his extensive field work he was able to reshape the chronology of Australia's prehistory and advance our knowledge of the Aboriginal culture.

Rhys Jones belongs to a group of several young archaeologists, many of them Cambridge-trained, who took up positions in Australia as part of the expansion of universities there in the 1960s. This period saw an explosion of knowledge in Australian archaeology as archaeologists tackled questions such as the age of human settlement, the impact of people on the environment and the role of ethnography in interpreting the past. The relatively new technique of radiocarbon dating dramatically extended the beginnings of Aboriginal occupation of Australia from 10,000 to 40,000 years ago in just over a decade of research. Rhys Jones's contribution to answering these questions cannot be overstated. He was also an excellent teacher and an eloquent communicator.

Jones was born into a Welsh-speaking family in north Wales, attended grammar school in Cardiff and went on to read Natural Sciences and Archaeology at Cambridge University. He took up a Teaching Fellowship at the University of Sydney

Below Jones's observations of modern Aboriginal life helped to inform his interpretations of their prehistory.

in 1963, where he completed a PhD Jones then moved to the Research School of Pacific Studies at the Australian National University in 1969, where he would spend the remainder of his career.

Tasmania and Arnhem Land

Jones's first field research in Australia focused on Tasmania, where his excavations at the Rocky Cape site confirmed that occupation there predated the separation of Tasmania from the mainland due to rising sea levels. He also conducted a study, via their records, of the early French explorers' encounters with Tasmanian hunter-gatherers. Jones's fascination with the Tasmanian story and the tragedy of their encounter with European society led to a collaboration with Tom Hayden on the film *The Last Tasmanian*.

In the 1980s Jones also played a key role in the discovery of an Ice Age occupation in south-west Tasmania and successfully campaigned to save these important sites from being drowned by the damming of the Franklin River for hydroelectric power.

In Arnhem Land (Northern Territory) he worked with his long-term partner and fellow archaeologist Betty Meehan, documenting the lives of the Anbarra people of the Blyth River area. From them he gained an insight into Aboriginal life and culture. The use of ethnography as a source of models for interpreting the historical past strongly informed his work.

Much of Rhys Jones's work focused on broad questions of chronology and also on the impact of human colonization on the Australian environment. He promoted the development of new dating methods based on luminescence, resulting in claims for the age of Australian human colonization as far back as 60,000 years and establishing the age of rock art through dating the sediments trapped in mud wasps' nests.

Firestick farming

Jones studied the issues of Aboriginal transformation of the natural environment through the use of fire, and developed the concept of 'firestick farming'. He first coined the term in 1969 after he observed how the Aborigines used controlled burnings to clear land for hunting and to change the local plant species. Firestick farming symbolized a change in attitude to Aboriginal people, and hunter-gatherers in general, as active managers of their environment, rather than random wanderers at the mercy of nature.

He had a flair for the dramatic, once famously announcing his land claim over Stonehenge as a Welshman and thus an indigenous person and true descendant of the builders of the sacred

British place. He believed passionately in the importance of Australian archaeology, both in terms of its contribution to the broader human story and the potential it held for the development of important theories in the study of hunter-gatherer societies. He made full use of the media and film to project his knowledge of Aboriginal studies and succeeded in putting Australian archaeology firmly on the international stage.

He died on 19 September 2001 at the age of 60 and was buried at Bungendore cemetery wearing his well-worn bushman's hat.

Kathleen Kenyon

(1906-1978)

An eminent British archaeologist of the ancient Near East whose excavations at Jericho during the 1950s made landmark discoveries, especially for early Neolithic periods. She also excavated at Samaria and Jerusalem, and published influential studies of Levantine archaeology.

Kathleen Kenyon was born in London on 5 January 1906, the daughter of Frederic Kenyon, a biblical scholar of high reputation, director of the British Museum and president of the British Academy. This background clearly influenced her choice of future career. She read history at Somerville College, Oxford, where she became the first woman president of the Oxford University Archaeological Society.

She gained her first archaeological experience in 1929 when she worked as a photographer on Gertrude Caton-Thompson's famous expedition to Great Zimbabwe in Africa.

During the 1930s Kenyon devoted much of her time to Roman Britain: she was a regular participant in the excavations carried out by Mortimer and Tessa Wheeler at Verulamium (St Albans), and she conducted her own

excavations at Jewry Wall (Leicester). Kenyon also assisted the Wheelers in establishing, in 1934, the famed Institute of Archaeology at the University of London. Mortimer Wheeler was at this time developing and applying his method of careful stratigraphic excavation (exploring a site in strata), and Kenyon's association with him deeply influenced her own approach to archaeological excavation.

During World War II Kenyon served as a divisional commander of the Red Cross, in Hammersmith, London, and also as the acting director of the Institute of Archaeology. When she resumed archaeological field work after the war, Kenyon initially pursued her Roman interests, with work in Britain and in Libya. But she soon launched the work in the Near East that would make her famous.

Apprenticeship at Samaria

Kenyon had received initial experience in the field of Near Eastern archaeology in the early 1930s, when she assisted in the excavations headed by John Crowfoot at Samaria, the capital of the biblical kingdom of Israel. The site had been heavily destroyed at the end of the 8th

Left Kenyon's work at Jericho took her back to the very beginnings of human civilization. The Pre-Pottery Neolithic stone tower dates to c.8000 BC. The tower, built of solid stone and standing 9m (30ft) high, was entered through an internal staircase.

century BC and then reoccupied through Roman times – its stratigraphy was very challenging. Kenyon's contribution to that project was a stratigraphic section through the site that extended from the Iron Age II (c.1000-600 BC) through the Roman periods.

Ancient Jericho

After the war Kenyon returned to the Near East where she was involved in the reopening of the British School of Archaeology in Jerusalem. Such is Kenyon's place in the life of this centre of learning that in July 2003 the British School was officially renamed the Kenyon Institute.

In 1952 Kenyon launched excavations at Jericho (Tell al-Sultan), which she continued until 1958. Jericho, a mound in a spring-fed oasis west of the Jordan river, had been the object of excavations by John Garstang during the 1930s. Kenyon's thorough excavations produced results that far exceeded those of the earlier work, making landmark contributions to regional and even world archaeology.

She exposed a Pre-Pottery Neolithic (roughly 8300-6200 BC) settlement protected by a massive stone wall and tower – a very early example of the coordination of community labour. The plastered skulls and plaster statues at the site were part of a mortuary cult characteristic of the period.

The subsequent Pottery Neolithic period (c.5800-4500 BC) levels contained pit houses, as well as pottery that helped elucidate this still poorly known period. The Early Bronze Age (mid-3rd millennium BC) town had been surrounded by a wall with towers, while the Middle Bronze Age (c.2000-1550 BC) town had been enclosed by earthen ramparts. Cemeteries situated around the mound contained collective burials in caves, the mortuary assemblages of which helped to refine significantly the chronology of Bronze Age material culture.

A Jerusalem finale

After Jericho Kenyon shifted her attention to Jerusalem, where she carried out the first modern excavation in the 'City of David' just south of Temple Mount. Begun in 1961 and brought to a close by the 1967 Six-Day War, the Jerusalem excavations must be counted as less successful than those at Jericho. Kenyon did find remains of the Iron Age II (1000-600 BC) capital of Judah, including traces of the town wall and of houses constructed on terraces up the hill slope, and also remains of later periods of occupation. However, these results are largely superseded by the work of Israeli archaeologists, who have been conducting many further excavations since 1967.

An influential figure

Kenyon's contribution to Near Eastern archaeology was not limited to the technical publication of results that are a necessary conclusion to any field project. She also wrote important overviews of Levantine archaeology, such as *Archaeology of the Holy Land* (1960), which helped shape a framework and questions that are still pertinent today. In addition, she encouraged several generations of budding archaeologists with her *Beginning in Archaeology* (1952), in which she explained the techniques and goals of archaeological field work. Other publications include: *Jerusalem - Excavating 3000 Years of History* (1967) and *Royal Cities of the Old Testament* (1971). In 1962 she was appointed Principal of St Hugh's College, Oxford and on her retirement in 1973 was made a Dame of the British Empire. Kathleen Kenyon died on 24 August 1978, in Wrexham, Wales.

Below A statue, fitted with remarkable shell eyes, from Jericho, dated to the 7th millennium BC. Kenyon also discovered plaster models made by sculpting the plaster over human skulls (these proved difficult to excavate).

The Leakey Family

(1903-present)

The Leakey family has had a huge impact not only on archaeology, but also on the general understanding of how the human species has evolved. Several generations of Leakeys have conducted research in Africa, exploring finds related to early human and proto-human life.

Louis and Mary Leakey formed a legendary partnership in the history of African archaeology and in the founding of the modern science of palaeoanthropology. The Leakey name is synonymous with human origins research in East Africa, though the couple's contributions also shaped many adjacent fields of academic study, such as primatology.

African investigation

Kenyan-born Louis Leakey (1903-1972) studied archaeology and anthropology at Cambridge University, graduating in 1926. Suspecting that Africa was the cradle of human evolution, he returned to East Africa and began seeking hominid fossils. He later met Mary Douglas (1913-1996), an English archaeologist and illustrator, whom he married in 1937. In early work, Louis Leakey explored the existing idea that Africa had experienced intermittent wet periods (known as pluvials) that corresponded to the European Ice Ages. In this model, culture and change were explained by correlating archaeological industries and sequences and palaeoclimatic episodes.

The popularity of the pluvial hypothesis waned, and Louis devoted himself to palaeoanthropological studies. There were few early

breakthroughs, but in 1948 the couple made a notable find near Lake Victoria of an 18-20 million-year-old Miocene primate named *Proconsul africanus*. It is not ancestral to humans, but its discovery heralded remarkable future finds, assisted by what became known as 'Leakey's luck'.

Olduvai Gorge

Work in Olduvai Gorge, in northern Tanzania, focused world attention on the Leakeys' quest for human origins. Olduvai is a ravine 48km (30 miles) long and 91m (300ft) deep. Partly an ancient lake basin, it is made up of a

series of beds, representing a build-up of layers of lava, volcanic ash and water-borne sediments. The hominid fossil-bearing beds had accumulated over approximately 2 million years.

Assuming that different artefact cultures might be associated with different early human species, the Leakeys set out to find the fossil remains of the makers of the stone-tool industries found in Olduvai Gorge. Correlating hominid species and artefacts recalls the idea of the 'pluvial hypothesis', in which cultural materials were linked to climatic episodes. Mary Leakey meticulously

Right Meave Leakey (b.1942) has continued the family tradition of African research. Her work in the Turkana Basin in Kenya produced some of the oldest surviving hominid remains.

classified the Olduvai artefactual industries as the Oldowan, Developed Oldowan and Early Acheulean.

The Olduvai Gorge work bore fruit in 1959 when Mary discovered a hominid cranium in Bed II. They named it *Zinjanthropus boisei* (in honour of Charles Boise, whose funding had enabled the work). *Zinjanthropus*, now known as *Australopithecus boisei*, was a robust (heavily built) species of australopithecine (a species of extinct hominid). It is now known that it lived in different East African locations between 2.3 and 1.2 million years ago.

At the time of the discovery, scientists believed that humans had most likely evolved in Asia, and at a much later date. The australopithecines are now regarded by most palaeoanthropologists to have been in the direct line of human ancestry. However, neither Louis, Mary nor their son Richard, also an eminent palaeoanthropologist, endorsed this interpretation. The excitement generated by the discovery of 'Zinj' attracted funding from the National Geographic Society, which allowed the Leakeys to continue and deepen their important research.

In 1960 their searches revealed a mandible and other bones that came to be named *Homo habilis* ('handy man'). The Leakeys believed this was the first tool-making hominid and probably a direct human ancestor. It may have given rise to *Homo erectus* fossils, another species found at Olduvai. (Early African specimens are also named *H. ergaster*.)

In time, Richard Leakey's team at Koobi Fora and Lake Turkana would reveal many more *H. ergaster* specimens, as well as individuals of a species named *Homo rudolfensis*, contemporary with *H. habilis*. Anatomical studies aside, the existence at Olduvai of in situ (undisturbed) materials, including 'home bases' and butchery locations, has been proposed but also contested. Such sites offer opportunities for investigating early human behaviour and society.

Fossil footprints

In later years Mary remained in East Africa with her beloved dalmatians while Louis travelled the world, giving lectures and raising essential funding. Louis died in 1972. Mary continued working in East Africa and in 1976-77 made a unique and important find. A volcanic eruption approximately 3.6 million years ago,

Left An anthropologist examines Laetoli footprints during a 1995 excavation. The hominid prints discovered at Laetoli were accompanied by dozens of animal prints.

Above The Olduvai gorge has produced a wide range of rich archaeological finds, ranging from 2.3 million to 15,000 years old.

at Laetoli in northern Tanzania, had rained ash over two, and probably three, sets of footprints – perhaps 70 prints in all. Initially stamped in soft ground, they were preserved by the hardening ash. Scientific examination suggested a pattern of movement and weight-transference characteristic of a creature walking upright. Mary believed they were made by early *Homo*, but most now attribute them to *Australopithecus afarensis* – the same species as the famous 'Lucy' – from Ethiopia. The significance of the Laetoli footprints lies in the light the find may shed on human evolution. Formerly it had been thought that the hominids before *Homo* had not been bipedal and that tool use may have preceded upright walking techniques.

The Leakey legacy

Though best known for their East African discoveries, and their many books and monographs, the Leakeys' influence went further. Studies by the primatologists Jane Goodall, Dian Fossey and Birute Galdikas-Brindamour of chimpanzees, gorillas and orang-utans, respectively, were made possible by Louis Leakey's support. Mary Leakey is also remembered for recording Tanzanian rock art, dating to the more recent African past. She diligently worked on, almost until her death in 1996 at the age of 83.

The Leakeys' studies have helped many researchers to rethink existing ideas about a single line of human descent. Instead, it seems that some of the hominid species had evolved in parallel with each other. Most of all, their work truly established the importance of Africa as the place where our species evolved.

The work of the Leakey family in the field of human evolution is perpetuated by the Leakey Foundation and by scores of independent and associated international researchers. They include Richard Leakey's wife, Meave, whose work has brought new species of hominid to light and, most recently, their daughter Louise.

Below The skull of Australopithecus boisei, discovered at the Olduvai Gorge, Tanzania.

André Leroi-Gourhan

(1911-1986)

Leroi-Gourhan's abiding interest was in the Palaeolithic period, particularly in the study of cave art. He saw a sophistication in the distribution of art around a cave not previously observed, and he produced one of the defining books on the interpretion of this primitive art form.

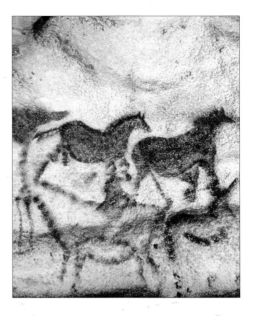

Above Leroi-Gourhan interpreted Palaeolithic art as structured and composed, rather than as a random collection of images.

André Leroi-Gourhan was a French archaeologist who made enormously important contributions to the excavation of Palaeolithic sites as well as to the study of Ice Age art. Born in Paris in 1911, he spent his early student years learning Russian and Chinese, after which he turned to ethnology and archaeology. He was involved in setting up Paris's Musée de l'Homme, of which he was a sub-director, and he was later professor at the Collège de France (1969-82).

Leroi-Gourhan carried out many major excavations, first in the caves of Arcy-sur-Cure — where he discovered the first known examples of ornaments made by Neanderthals — and subsequently at the late Ice Age open-air site of Pincevent near Paris, a camp of reindeer hunters. Here he pioneered techniques of horizontal excavation, the minute study and moulding of occupation floors, and ethnological reconstruction of the life of stone-age people.

Interpreting cave art

Leroi-Gourhan's huge book *Préhistoire de l'Art Occidental* (1965) embodied his revolutionary approach to Palaeolithic art. Previously, cave art had been seen as simple accumulations of figures (most notably by the Abbé Breuil) and interpreted through simplistic use of supposed analogies to modern cultures. Leroi-Gourhan, together with Annette Laming, strove to avoid such analogies, and saw the figures as purposefully arranged within each cave. He found that horses and bison dominated the art numerically, and tended to cluster in the central parts of the caves. He believed that horses were male symbols, and bison female, even when the bisons were clearly bulls.

Leroi-Gourhan was also the first to tackle the enigmatic 'signs' in Palaeolithic art, deciding that, like the animal figures, they constituted a dual system for exploring and explaining the world, which might perhaps be interpreted in the sexual terms of vulvar signs and phallic signs.

Subsequent work inevitably modified or cast doubt on much of this approach, but it nevertheless remains the single greatest contribution to the interpretation of Palaeolithic art.

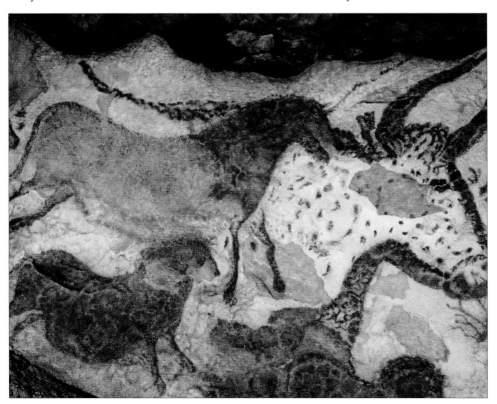

Left A detail from one of the reproduction cave paintings at Lascaux II, a facsimile site opened in France in 1983.

Spyridon Marinatos

(1901-1974)

A Greek archaeologist with an international reputation, Marinatos excavated several famous sites of the Aegean. One of his greatest finds was the remains of an ancient Minoan city entombed beneath volcanic rock on Thera, wiped out by a cataclysmic volcanic eruption around 1500 BC.

Spyridon Marinatos was born on the Greek island of Kefalonia on 4 November 1901, a time when the earlier discovery of Mycenae and Knossos had heightened world interest in archaeology. At the age of 19, while still an undergraduate reading archaeology at Athens University, he was appointed an inspector of antiquities.

In 1929, after postgraduate study in Germany at Berlin and Halle, he became director of the Archaeological Museum of Heraklion, Crete. Here his excavations at the Villa of the Lilies (so called because fragments of frescoes found there depicted red and white lilies), and other buildings in the nearby settlement of Amnissos, gave him a valuable first-hand experience of Minoan archaeology.

The Thera volcano

Like other Minoan sites on Crete, Amnissos had been struck by an earthquake, then rebuilt, and was later mysteriously abandoned after a fire. Pumice found in a seafront building is said to have led Marinatos to think of the Cyclades island of Thera – modern Santorini – situated 100km (62 miles) to the north of Crete, which had been torn apart by a massive volcanic eruption. In 1939 Marinatos published in the journal *Antiquity* his theory that this eruption had actually taken place around 1500 BC, and had caused such devastation that it had brought about the demise of the flourishing Minoan civilization.

Marinatos proposed excavating on Santorini where, during the late 1800s, artefacts had been exposed by minor earthquakes and during quarrying. French, German and Greek archaeologists had dug around the village of Akrotiri, exposing the remains of ancient buildings. However, the outbreak of World War II and then the Greek Civil War made work impossible and Marinatos busied himself with other projects. In 1946 he travelled abroad in search of antiquities stolen by occupying forces, and during the 1950s he excavated the Minoan settlement and palace complex at Vathypetro, Crete, where he found a wine and olive press and a potter's kiln. Intending to turn Vathypetro into a museum, Marinatos had the remains reconstructed, for which he was criticized by his peers, since this made further excavation and interpretation difficult.

Left A view of the ancient city of Akrotiri, Thera, as it has emerged from the volcanic rock. Despite its great age, the site has been impressively preserved, with many staircases still standing alongside numerous pithoi (storage jars) and the framework of a sophisticated drainage system.

Excavating Akrotiri

Geologists had been sceptical about Marinatos's 1939 theories, arguing that earthquakes occurring on Santorini were never as powerful as he claimed. In the 1960s, however, American scientists from Columbia University found thick ash deposits in ooze that was dredged up from the Mediterranean. The ash was found to be from the Thera volcano and it covered so vast an area that the eruption that produced it must have been of the magnitude of the 1883 eruption of Krakatoa, Indonesia. Interest revived and in 1967 the Greek Archaeological Society licensed Marinatos, then General Inspector of Antiquities, to excavate on Santorini near the village of Akrotiri.

Marinatos's team chose a point on the southern tip of the island, where the tephra (solidified ash) was thinnest, and at about 30m (98ft) they uncovered streets, squares, multi-storey dwellings and workshops of the most important Minoan port outside Crete. The earliest pipes and water closets ever discovered showed that the port was inhabited by an advanced civilization that used cold water and hot (from thermal springs). Jars in ancient storerooms contained traces of olive oil and other food – but there were no skeletons, indicating that people had prior warning of the eruption and had fled.

Some of the dwellings excavated at Akrotiri displayed delicate, well-preserved Minoan frescoes. One depicts saffron-gatherers presenting their harvest of stamens to a seated figure, perhaps a goddess. In another two youths are shown boxing.

From 1968 Marinatos published annual reports of his findings at Akrotiri. His team uncovered just a corner of Akrotiri, however, and excavations continue to this day. Geologists have also recovered evidence that suggests that the Thera

Right One of the most beautiful frescoes at Akrotiri is this young fisherman holding his catch on a string.

eruption may have been many times the magnitude of Krakatoa, creating a dust cloud so great that it blocked out the sun for a prolonged period.

Marinatos also made other highly significant excavations that yielded important archaeological finds. In 1966 he unsuccessfully searched the seafloor for the fabled drowned city of Helike, but in the early 1970s he located the site of the Battle of Thermopylae and excavated the ancient burial mound constructed after the Battle of Marathon.

Marinatos was killed in an accident at Akrotiri in October 1974 when an ancient wall collapsed on him. At the site a fitting memorial marks his immeasurable contribution to the archaeology of the Aegean.

Harald Pager

(1923-1985)

Harald Pager was one of the most accomplished and dedicated rock art researchers of our time. His name is synonymous with Ndedema Gorge in southern Africa where he uncovered and meticulously recorded thousands of cave paintings.

Born and brought up in a small town in Czechoslovakia, Harald Pager settled in Austria after World War II, where he trained as an industrial designer and artist at an art college in Graz.

He emigrated to South Africa in 1956 where he worked as a commercial artist before embarking upon the recording of rock art made by the San (Bushmen), a Stone Age hunter-gatherer people.

Ndedema Gorge

In 1971 Pager's work was published in a large volume entitled *Ndedema*. This work is perhaps the most significant book on rock art ever produced. It documented five years' work with his wife Shirley-Ann, who always assisted him, locating and recording the rock paintings of one richly painted valley – Ndedema (now known as Didima) – in the Drakensberg Moutains, KwaZulu-Natal, South Africa. The couple found 17 sites in the 5.5-km (3.4-mile) long valley and meticulously recorded each of the almost 4000 individual images painted on the walls of the rock shelters.

The work was a milestone in South African rock-art research. Only in the 1950s had A.R. Willcox effectively and systematically first used colour photography in recording. Previously, recorders had relied on freehand drawings, watercolour copies and, later, monochrome photographs.

Only photography, with its total faithfulness to detail, reproduced the all-important details of the rock face, and only colour reproductions conveyed the palette on which the images rely for their visual impact. Pager, who was both visually and scientifically trained, recognized that colour photography was problematic in recording less well-preserved images. To accommodate this, he developed an innovative technique that entailed first photographing the paintings in black and white. The couple then returned to the site and painted onto the photographs with oil paints, which were carefully colour-matched.

Professor Raymond Dart's enthusiastic foreword to *Ndedema* hailed the book as the 'first and only' publication to be directly modelled on archaeological and scientific principles. Pager's precision recording included plotting every mark and compiling quantitative data, not only on subject matter but also on composition, perspective, technique and postures. The quantitative data are

Left Harald Pager at work copying a panel of three tall hunters and eland (Africa's largest antelope) at Botha's Shelter, Ndedema Gorge. The pigments used in the cave paintings were mainly black, white and orange, although there is great depth in this palette.

integrated into a detailed discussion of the archaeology of the Drakensberg San peoples and the environment of the region. Colour plates and line drawings of true virtuoso quality complete the tour de force.

Before relocating to Namibia, Pager published another important book on South African rock art, *Stone Age Myth and Magic*, comprising an extended discussion of the significance of the paintings.

Pager and rock art

Today, some researchers question the value of science for understanding art and culture. However, though in *Ndedema* Pager chose to suspend the question of aesthetics, his appreciation of visuality underpinned his approach. The shamanistic model, which subsequently emerged, reverted to analysing the art almost exclusively in terms of subject matter. That model has been widely criticized, for example by art historians, better equipped than anthropologists to appreciate Pager's close attention to the visual characteristics of the rock paintings.

Pager's visual acuity, and his vast and empathetic familiarity with the materials, enhanced his insights into San rock-art traditions. He was, for example, sceptical of the claim that the imagery derived from the hallucinations of 'shamans', noting that the shamanistic explanation was insufficiently tied to the paintings themselves and their visual attributes.

Namibian rock art

In 1978 Pager embarked on another, perhaps even more, ambitious recording programme, this time in the Brandberg Mountains, Namibia. There, together with two Namibian field assistants, he recorded nearly 900 sites containing over 40,000 figures. Five volumes have been

Right A crowded panel from Sebaaini Shelter, Ndedema Gorge. Many paintings are superimposed on other older paintings. There were 1146 paintings in all at the site when Harald Pager was there to copy them.

published so far, covering the Amis Gorge, Hungorob Gorge, the Southern Gorges, Umuab and Karuab Gorges, Naib Gorge and the Northwest. Regrettably, the economics of publishing demanded reliance on line drawings rather than colour reproductions, but Pager's efforts have nevertheless resulted in a truly monumental record of the colour and vibrancy of Namibian art.

Harald Pager died prematurely in 1985. Though remembered for his recording, his legacy lies also in the domains of conservation and in raising awareness of African rock arts.

Tatiana Proskouriakoff

(1909-1985)

Proskouriakoff was one of the 20th century's pioneering researchers into Maya peoples and cultures. Training as an architectural artist enabled her to bring ruins to life in her published work, while her new interpretation of Maya hieroglyphics changed the way inscriptions are studied.

Born in Tomsk, Siberia, on 23 January 1909, Tatiana Proskouriakoff moved to the United States in 1916 where her chemist father was posted to oversee munitions production for the Russian war effort. She received a Bachelor of Science in Architecture from Pennsylvania State University in 1930. Lack of work as an architect during the Depression led her to take a job as illustrator at the university museum.

First expedition

Her work at the museum attracted the attention of archaeologist Linton Satterthwaite, who invited her to join his 1936 expedition to the site of Piedras Negras, Guatemala. So began her illustrious career as ethnologist and archaeologist. During her time at Piedras Negras, Proskouriakoff would create some of the best-known archaeological reconstructive drawings from sites all over the Maya world.

While studying the hieroglyphic inscriptions on monuments at Piedras Negras, Proskouriakoff noticed a repetitive pattern of dates and signs which she identified as a succession of seven rulers spanning 200 years. From this she demonstrated that Maya texts spoke of rites of passage and the major accomplishments of rulers, rather than – as had previously been believed – purely astronomical and calendrical knowledge. This work, on which current knowledge of epigraphy (study of inscriptions) is based, won

Above A Maya stela (carved stone slab) from Piedras Negras. Many of the stone carvings depicted either rulers or local deities.

Proskouriakoff the Alfred V. Kidder Medal (which she herself had designed) in 1962.

Over the course of her career, Proskouriakoff published numerous pioneering works, including *An Album of Maya Architecture* (1946), *A Study of Classic Maya Sculpture* (1950), *Portraits of Women in Maya Art* (1961) and *Jades from the Cenote of Sacrifice, Chichén Itzá, Yucatan* (1974). In addition to the Kidder Medal, she was awarded Pennsylvania State Woman of the Year (1971), honorary degrees from Tulane University and Pennsylvania State University, and the prestigious Order of the Quetzal from the people of Guatemala (1984). Her friends and family remember her as a disciplined scholar and free-spirited individual, who was not afraid to follow her ideas and contradict those of her colleagues. She died on 30 August 1985.

Left Maya hieroglyphs on a stela from Tikal, Guatemala. The complex writing system is made up of hundreds of unique signs, or glyphs, in the form of humans, animals, supernaturals, objects and abstract designs.

Maria Reiche

(1903-1998)

For over 50 years the German-born Maria Reiche devoted her life to exploring the Nasca lines in Peru. Her work revealed some of the secrets of the lines, while also helping to preserve this amazing archaeological phenomenon for future generations.

No major archaeological site is perhaps more closely linked with a single name and personality than the Nasca (Nazca) lines of Peru. These huge lines form designs etched into the desert between the Nasca and Ingenio river valleys, several hours'

Left This glyph of a dog is one of the most complex of the Nasca figures.

drive south of Lima. They would almost certainly have been destroyed long ago had it not been for the work of Maria Reiche.

Reiche was born in Dresden, Germany, in 1903. Her father, a judge, died in World War I, and her mother, who had studied in England as well as Berlin, taught and did other work to support the family. Reiche spoke and read several languages, and she studied mathematics at Hamburg and Dresden and became a teacher. In 1932 she left Germany to accept a position as governess to a family in Cuzco, Peru, later moving to Lima where she made a living teaching and working as a translator at San Marcos University. It was through her academic connections there that she was eventually drawn to Nasca.

Desert lines

The Nasca lines had been virtually unknown until commercial air traffic began in Peru during the 1920s. Pilots for Faucett, the first company to run flights between Lima and the southern city of Arequipa, noticed huge lines, triangles and other markings on the desert pampa to the north of the town of Nasca.

The Peruvian archaeologist Toribio Mejía Xesspe conducted the first formal study of the lines in 1927, publishing an article in which he suggested that the lines were ancient ceremonial pathways. In 1941 the American historian Paul Kosok, who had come to Peru to study ancient irrigation canal systems and the origins of Andean civilization, became interested in the Nasca lines. He observed that some of the lines

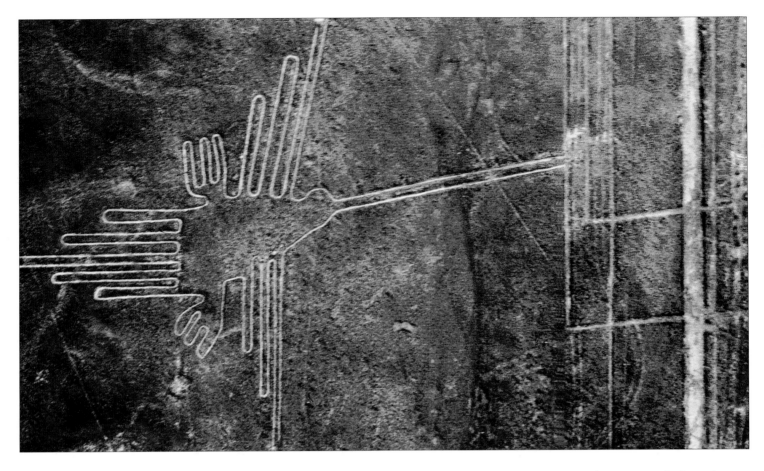

Above An aerial photograph of the outline of a hummingbird. Like other Nasca lines, it can be recognized as a coherent figure only from the air.

marked the winter solstice from a central location and theorized that the lines might have been used to make astronomical and calendrical observations. Kosok had hired Reiche to make translations for him, and he inspired her to begin researching the Nasca lines in her own right.

The Nasca lines consist of a huge complex of gigantic figures etched into the surface of the desert across nearly 40km (25 miles) of the south coast of Peru. Most of the lines form geometric designs, including loops, triangles and other forms, but some 30 or so of the designs on the Nasca plain itself are figures, mostly animals.

The many lines were made by removing rocks and sand that had been blackened by centuries of exposure to the elements (forming the surface known as 'desert varnish'), leaving lighter coloured lines on the surface of the plain. The designs, and the pottery associated with the lines, indicate that they were made by the ancient Nasca, a civilization known for its spectacular polychrome pottery and masterful use of underground water resources for irrigation of the desert. The Nasca culture thrived during what is known as the Early Intermediate Period, beginning roughly 2000 years ago and lasting for approximately 600 or 700 years.

Left The Nasca monkey with its huge spiral tail was first recognized by Maria Reiche in 1946. Such is the scale of the artworks, that they probably took several hundred years to complete.

A life's work

Reiche's work on the Nasca lines began after the end of World War II, when she was allowed to move freely in Peru after a period of severe restrictions on German citizens ended. She spent virtually all of her remaining years living there, mostly in primitive conditions, studying the lines and working for their preservation. Although she received some funding, and occasional support (particularly in the area of aerial photography) from the Peruvian military, plus the attention of scholars and intellectuals inside and outside of Peru, she worked largly alone. She battled to save the lines from destruction due to increasing traffic from the Panamerican highway and other development. Peru's National Cultural Institute declared the lines an intangible zone in 1970, laying an important foundation for their protection. It was Maria Reiche, however, who hired and paid the guards that protected the lines.

Regarded for many years as a somewhat eccentric foreigner by the local people, Reiche eventually became a revered member of the community as tourism, based largely on the fame of the lines, began to take off in the 1970s. She spent the latter years of her life installed in the relative luxury of the Tourist Hotel in Nasca, becoming one of its major attractions herself. By the 1980s she was suffering from glaucoma and Parkinson's disease, but she continued to give daily lectures to visitors and to advocate her theory that the lines had been made by Nasca astronomers to mark major calendrical events.

Maria Reiche believed strongly in her own theories of the Nasca lines, paying little attention to the work of other scholars, and she saved the lines and carefully documented them. Scientific studies of the lines have demonstrated that some do mark major calendrical events, such as the summer and winter solstice, but many do not. Current theories about their significance focus on Andean cosmology and posit that some may have served to guide pilgrimages, ceremonial processions and other rituals. The lines have drawn the interest of scientists and pseudo-scientists for the past 50 years. Although many scholars disagree with Reiche's theories about the purpose of the lines, they all acknowledge that without her they would not be there today for us to study.

Above The Nasca lines, including this impressive parrot, were declared a UNESCO World Heritage Site in 1995.

Below The surface of the Nasca desert (one of the driest in the world) consists of rock, not sand, hence the Nasca lines have been preserved.

John Howland Rowe

(1918-2004)

His total dedication to accurate research and his vast knowledge of the history of South America made John Rowe a world authority on Andean culture and history. His seminal 1946 paper on the Inca at the time of the Spanish Conquest remains an international standard reference.

John Howland Rowe is one of the most important figures in the development of Andean archaeology as an academic discipline in the United States. His work is likely to have a deep and lasting importance over archaeological debate for years to come. While many American archaeologists focused on field work and techniques of analysis in archaeology, and worked in multiple areas applying basically similar approaches to different regions, Rowe emphasized a different approach – deep expertise in a single region. Furthermore, instead of applying one academic approach to multiple regions or sites, he applied approaches from multiple disciplines – including archaeology, history and linguistics – to the study of the Andean past, and especially to the history of the Inca. Unsurpassed in his knowledge of the Inca for more than a generation, his

Below The carved rock 'Inca throne', one of the key features of the Inca temple (or fortress) overlooking Cuzco at Sacsayhuaman, Peru.

interpretations of Inca history and archaeology formed the basis for virtually all research on the Inca in the late 20th century.

Beginnings

Rowe stated that he had been interested in archaeology from the time he was three years old. He was born on 10 June 1918, in Sorrento, Maine. His father, Louis Earl Rowe, had spent a single field season in Egypt, an experience that left him with a lifelong interest in the ancient past which he passed on to his son.

John Rowe studied classical archaeology at Brown University before moving to Harvard to study anthropology, receiving his master's degree in 1941. From there he went to Peru, where he conducted research and taught in Cuzco before serving with the US Combat Engineers in Europe between 1944 and 1946. He later returned to Harvard, where he received his Ph.D. in Latin American History and Anthropology in 1947. Rowe was hired by the University of California at Berkeley in 1948 and he spent the rest of his career there, teaching and building the anthropology library at one of the premier anthropology departments in the United States.

Rowe's scholarship was greatly influenced by his background in classical studies. The study of classical archaeology required proficiency in ancient languages, as well as in history, art styles and archaeology. Rowe's linguistic abilities and training enabled him to master Spanish easily and then to learn Quechua, the language of the Inca that was still widely spoken in Cuzco and other areas of Peru. He was also able to read and understand Spanish colonial records of many kinds. His application of art historical techniques of stylistic analysis led to a rigorous approach to definition and classification of the iconographic and artistic styles of archaeological cultures of the Andes, an approach that he passed on to his students.

Study method

Rowe believed in studying data in great detail. He read colonial documents thoroughly and assessed their relevance and also the accuracy of their information based on his knowledge of Inca history and archaeology. His reliance on historical evidence, and particularly on those sources that he viewed as reliable, led him to discredit many other previously well-regarded sources, or at least portions of what they said.

His most influential body of work is his description of Inca civilization before the Spanish conquest, as well as his interpretations of the impact of the Spanish on the indigenous culture during the early colonial era. His most widely read paper is called 'Inca Culture at the Time of the Spanish Conquest', published in the multi-volume *Handbook of South American Indians* in 1946. In this and related works, Rowe synthesized his knowledge and interpretations of Inca civilization and provided a picture of Inca society that scholars, tour guides and interested lay persons could grasp.

A lasting contribution

Rowe left an important legacy to archaeology in the students he trained both in the United States and Peru, the scholarly organization he founded, with its academic journal dedicated to Andean studies, and the anthropology library he founded at the University of California. His scholarly papers and editorial productions number more than 300 from 1940 to 2005, with a large proportion in Spanish.

His emphasis on detailed knowledge and deep understanding of the available data set high standards that have helped Andean archaeology to grow as a discipline. His interpretations of the Inca remain important, even as the details of the Inca civilization are clarified and modified by new research. Rowe retired in 1988, but continued research work until his death in Berkeley in 2004.

Below A figurine depicting one of the 'chosen women' (often called 'Virgins of the Sun'), who were concubines of the Inca emperor and given to seal political marriage alliances between Inca and other societies.

Sir J. Eric Thompson

(1898-1975)

The English archaeologist John Eric Sidney Thompson is widely regarded as the pre-eminent scholar of the pre-Columbian Maya civilization of the first half of the 20th century. He made a lasting contribution to the decipherment of Maya.

Above A detail of a carving at the ruined Maya city of Coba. Thompson published a detailed description of the site in 1932.

Thompson was born in London on 31 December 1898. He was sent to Winchester College in 1912, but at the outbreak of World War I he joined the army under the assumed name Neil Winslow, giving false information about his age. An injury ended his army career with the Coldstream Guards in 1918. After working as a gaucho in Argentina, he went on to study anthropology at Cambridge University.

Researching the Maya

In 1926 Thompson went to Chichén Itzá, Mexico, to work with the celebrated Mayanist Sylvanus Morley of the Carnegie Institution. During his time with the Institution, Thompson was sent to numerous sites around the Maya world. Most notable were his travels through the British Honduras (Belize). His work there involved some of the first excavations of smaller sites beyond elite ceremonial centres, focusing on the lives of 'common' Maya. During this time he also gathered information from many modern Maya people, recognizing the continuity of certain beliefs and practices that dated all the way back to pre-Hispanic times.

Thompson was also sent to the Maya site of Coba in Mexico, and his report of the large ruined city and its many hieroglyphic inscriptions prompted Sylvanus Morley to carry out a more thorough investivation of the remote site.

Thompson's work produced a correlation between the Maya calendar and the Gregorian calendar that remains in use to this day. During the 1940s he also conducted considerable work on the decipherment of Maya hieroglyphics, developing a numerical cataloguing system for the glyphs that survives in the modern discipline.

Thompson was a prolific writer and was passionate about transferring his knowledge to the wider world. His incredible corpus of respected publications includes *The Civilisation of the Mayas* (1927), *Ethnology of the Mayas of Southern and Central British Honduras* (1930), *Maya Hieroglyphic Writing: Introduction* (1950), *A Catalogue of Maya Hieroglyphs* (1962), *Maya History and Religion* (1970), and also an amusing autobiography entitled *Maya Archaeologist* (1963).

Thompson received many honours in recognition of his work and was knighted in 1975, shortly before his death in Cambridge that year.

Left An aerial view of the ruins at Coba. Thompson made his first visit through the jungle by mule while on his honeymoon.

Michael Ventris

(1922-1956)

By the time he was 30, Michael Ventris had deciphered Europe's oldest written language, which had been found half a century before in engravings on clay tablets at Knossos. He proved what experts had refused to consider: that Linear B writing was an archaic form of ancient Greek.

Michael Ventris was a 14-year-old schoolboy when he attended a lecture and exhibition on Minoan civilization given in London by the 86-year-old archaeologist Sir Arthur Evans. On display were tablets engraved with a script which, Ventris was told, no one could decipher. When excavating Knossos, the Minoan palace-complex on Crete, in 1901, Evans had excavated more than 3,000 tablets and had identified their faint engravings as writing. Evans distinguished a hieroglyphic script and two scripts composed of glyphs and other symbols, which he named 'Linear A' and 'Linear B'. Certain that they were examples of Minoan writing, Evans devoted the next several decades to their decipherment but to no avail.

Ventris, who had learned Polish from his mother, French and German during his childhood in Switzerland, and studied Latin and Greek at his English prep school, resolved to decode the hieroglyphics of Linear B. At 18 he published his first conclusions – that Linear B was the script of the Etruscans – in the *American Journal of Archaeology*, which aroused academic interest.

Background

Rather than read classics at university, however, Ventris trained as an architect, enrolling at the Architectural Association School of Architecture in 1940. In 1943, with World War II at its height, he joined the RAF and flew as a navigator but continued his professional training after the war. He also worked diligently on deciphering the elusive Linear B in his spare time.

Leaps in the dark

An American philologist Alice Kober had already prepared some of the groundwork for the decipherment of Linear B by working out a grid expressing the relationships between vowels and consonants in the script. After Kober's death in 1950, Ventris built on her work. Inspired guesses speeded his progress. For example, he assumed that the most common symbol was the vowel 'a'; that certain symbols followed by glyphs were women's names and others men's; and that commonly occurring symbols on the tablets found on Crete, but not on others excavated on the Greek mainland, were town names.

As he deciphered more of the hieroglyphics, Ventris noticed a connection between Linear B and the ancient Greek language. A link with Greek had been firmly rejected for 50 years, but in 1952 Ventris publicized this idea in a BBC talk. Afterwards, he received an offer of assistance from John Chadwick, a recognized specialist in archaic Greek.

The two men deciphered the tablets more completely and in 1953 they jointly published their conclusions: Linear B, they announced, was a written form of the ancient Greek used by the first Greeks – the Mycenaeans – and was used from around 1450 BC. The discovery met first with scepticism, then with acclaim. Yet for Ventris it marked the end of his obsession with Linear B.

Having solved the problem, his interest waned. He returned briefly to architecture but, dissatisfied with his achievements, soon abandoned it. Always a loner, he had little to fall back on: his marriage had failed; his children had become strangers. On 6 September 1956, he died in a car accident at the age of just 34.

Below A clay tablet from the Mycenaean Palace at Pylos, in Greece. The Linear B tablets revealed financial records and lists of livestock and agricultural produce, tableware, textiles and furniture.

INDEX

PICTURE CREDITS

akg-images 9b, 15t, 21, /ullstein bild 11r, 32t, 65r, 80t, /Erich Lessing 26b, 27b **Ancient Art and Architecture Collection** 14b, 28t and b, 52b, 71t, 74b, 75, 76t, 91b, /Danita Delimont, front cover tl, 41t /Prisma 27t, /G Tortoli 80b **The Art Archive** 8t and b, 12b, 47b, /Dagli Orti back 9t and r, 17t, /Bibliotheque des Arts Decoratifs, Paris/Dagli Orti 12t, 18b, /Musee du Louvre, Paris/Dagli Orti 14t, 55t, /Heraklion Mus./ Dagli Orti spine, 16m, 17b, /British Mus./ Dagli Orti 18t, /Musee des Antiques St Germain en Laye/Dagli Orti 23b, /National Archaeological Mus. Athens/Dagli Orti 29t, /Culver Pictures 39t, 40b, /Egyptian Mus. Cairo/ Dagli Orti 39b, 40t, 41b /Beijing Institute of Archaeology/Laurie Platt Winfrey 42m, /National Mus. Karachi/Dagli Orti 53t, /National Mus. Damascus/Dagli Orti 62m, /Archaeological Mus. Salonica/Dagli Orti 66t, 67b, /Mireille Vautier 68t, /Museo de las Culturas, Oaxaca/Dagli Orti 71b, /Museo di Anthropologia ed Etnografia, Turin/Dagli Orti 79b, /Archaeological Mus. Tikal, Guatemala/Dagli Orti 84b, /Rijksmuseum voor Volkenkunde, Leiden/Dagli Orti 94bl, /Mus. of

Anatolian Civilizations, Ankara/Dagli Orti **Paul Bahn** 23t **Bibliotheque de l'Ecole des mines de Paris** 22t **Bridgeman Art Library** Jacket: back flap; (both), front and back; tl, tml, tr, bml, br, front flap; tl Inside pages: 1, 2, 3, 4, 5bl **British School at Athens** 47t, 50t **The Cambridgeshire Collection, Cambridge Central Library and the Principal and Fellows, Newnham College, Cambridge** 44t **Corbis**: 26t, 30b, 48t, /Penny Tweedie 72-73, /epa/Eduardo Herran 85b, /Chris Lisle 27, 32b, /Jeremy Horner 58b, /Sygma/Pierre Vauthey 78b, /Hulton-Deutsch Collection 11l, 16t, 29b, 54t, 56t, /Historical Picture Archive 10, /Bettmann 13, 35m and r, 36, 38b, 42, 51t, 61t, 62t, 63m, 74t, 77t, 85t, /Nik Wheeler 19, /Roger Wood 20t and b, /Ted Spiegel 31b, /Reuters/Pilar Olivares 33t, /Hanan Isachar 44b, 45b, /Visions of America/Joseph Sohm 48b, /David Muench 49t, /Buddy Mays 49b, /Gianni Dagli Orti 51b, 84t, /Lindsay Hebberd 53b, /David Bartruff 57, /Charles and Josette Lenars 58b, 59b, /Kevin Schafer 59t, /Michael Freeman 64, /Sygma/ Robert Campbell 65l, 77b, /Richard A. Cooke back cover tr, 68b, /Danny

Lehman 69, /Archivo Iconografico, S.A. 70t, /Eric and David Hosking 79t, /Werner Forman 88t, /Peter M. Wilson 90t, /Yann-Arthus Bertrand 90b **Getty Images**: /Time Life Pictures 35l, 38t, 43t, 58t, /Roger Viollet 22b, /National Geographic 78, /Express/Hulton Archive 91t **David Gill** 66b, 69t **Latin American Library/Tulane University** 11m, 30t **Andrew McLeod** 5tl **Mus. of London Archaeology Service** 46t and b **Courtesy of Shirley Ann Pager** 82–83 **Pitt-Rivers Mus. University of Oxford** 25bm **Mr G. A. Pitt-Rivers. By kind permission of Salisbury and South Wiltshire Mus.** 24t and b, 25t and br **Robert Harding** 34, 52t, /John Ross 15b, /Vanderhart 42b, /Lorraine Wilson 50b, /Ursula Gahwiler 54b, /Michael Jenner 55b, /Adam Woolfitt 61b, /Richard Ashworth 63t, /Gina Corrigan 70b, /Gavin Hellier 81, /Odyssey 86b **The Wace Archive** 60 **Werner Forman Archive** Nick Saunders 36b, 37, 86t, 87t, 88b, /British Mus. London 62b, 63b, /National Mus. Copenhagen 31t, /Mus. fur Volkerkunde, Berlin 33b, /David Bernstein Fine Art, New York 89.